The 10 Seasc

BARNSLEY

Seasons 1983-84 to 1992-93

Season-by-Season Commentary
Keith Lodge
Sports Editor, Barnsley Chronicle

Statistics and History
Mike Ross

Editors
Michael Robinson, John Robinson & Philip Norminton

CONTENTS

British Library Cataloguing in Publication Data
A catalogue record for this book is available from the British Library
ISBN 0-947808-34-5

Copyright © 1993; SOCCER BOOK PUBLISHING LTD. (0472-696226)
72, St. Peters' Avenue, Cleethorpes, Sth. Humberside, DN35 8HU, England

Printed by Adlard Print & Typesetting Services, The Old School, The Green, Ruddington, Notts. NG11 6HH

BARNSLEY FIRSTS by Mike Ross

In 'The Book of Football', (published 1906) Mr.F.Lodge describes how a 'band of old schoolboys', playing under the title of 'Barnsley Wanderers' were the pioneers of the game in the town before the formation of Barnsley FC. Rugby was, apparently a strong force and, until the Rev. Tiverton Preedy, curate of St. Peter's Church, former Barnsley St. Peters in 1887, these 'Wanderers' were the town's sole representatives in the 'round-ball' game, playing other amateur teams in the Sheffield area.

Barnsley St. Peters, 1892
During their days of Sheffield League Football

Barnsley St. Peters rented their 'Oakwell' ground from Mr.Arthur Senior and played a number of games during their first year. The club's very first game was against a team called Manor House and was played at Worsborough Bridge on 17th September 1887. This game ended in a 4-0 victory for 'The Saints' (as they were then known) and the scorers were believed to have been Denton (2), Thompson and Chappell. Football blossomed in the town following the formation of 'The Saints' and, soon, because many clubs had come into existence, 'The Barnsley Football Union' was set up.

Barnsley first entered the F.A. Cup competition in 1893 when their opponents were one of the top sides of the day - Gainsborough Trinity. Playing at home, the club scored four goals (Stringer (2), Hirst and Smith) but still lost the tie 4-5!

By 1895 Barnsley were playing in the Midland League (the GM Vauxhall Conference of the day) and, within three years were elected into the Second Division of the Football League after winning the Championship. Even then most of their opponents were clubs which are still around today, and, indeed, their first game was against Lincoln City on 1st September 1898 which ended in a 0-1 defeat. The first victory followed a little over a week later when Luton Town were defeated 2-1. The club's first League goal was scored in this match by John McArtney who went on to become club secretary and manager before moving back to Scotland to take charge of St.Mirren.

Barnsley's F.A. Cup winning team
Players only (left to right, front row): Wilf Bartrop, Harry Tufnell, George Lillycrop, George Travers, Jimmy Moore
(left to right, 2nd row): Bob Glendenning, Dicky Downs, Jack Cooper, Archie Taylor, Phil Bratley, George Utley (far right is Will Norman, the trainer)

At the turn of the century 'St. Peters' was dropped from the name and the club colours which had been blue and white stripes were changed to red. In 1907 the club purchased the freehold of the Oakwell Ground for the princely sum of £1,376 and, three years later (although still a Second Division side) enjoyed a tremendous F.A. Cup run. Then, having beaten Everton 3-0 in the Semi-Final Replay (after drawing the first game 0-0) Barnsley reached the Final at Crystal Palace when their opponents were Newcastle United. This game also ended in a draw (1-1) and Barnsley then lost the replay 2-0. The club's F.A. Cup glory, however, was not over and two years later they reached the Final again, this time against West Bromwich Albion. Yet again, the match ended in a draw but the club went on to win the replay 1-0 to achieve Barnsley's greatest triumph.

The club remained in the Second Division until being relegated to the Third Division North in 1932 but, after winning the Championships two seasons later, returned to the Second Division one more. Since the War, Barnsley have had brief spells in both the Third and Fourth Divisions but are, nevertheless, reknowned for being one of the most consistent Second Division sides of all time.

CLUB FIRSTS

First Game & Win
as Barnsley St. Peters FC, 17th September 1887
vs Manor House (a) - score 4-0

First Scorer
Not Confirmed - scorers were Denton (2),
A. Thompson & R. Chappell

First F.A. Cup Game & F.A. Cup Defeat
14th October 1893 vs Gainsborough Trinity (h) -
score 4-5

First F.A. Cup Scorer
Not Confirmed - scorers were Stringer (2), Hirst
& Smith

First F.A. Cup Hat-Trick
3rd November 1898 vs Gainsborough Trinity (h) -
score 4-0. Scored by H. Davis (3)

First F.A. Cup Win
13th October 1894 vs Grantham (h) - score 3-1

First F.A. Cup Draw
24th November 1894 vs Mexborough (a) -
score 1-1

First F.A. Cup Semi-Final
1909-10 vs Everton - score 0-0 in first game,
3-0 in the replay

First F.A. Cup Final
23rd April 1910 vs Newcastle United - score 1-1
in first game, 0-2 in the replay

First F.A. Cup Final Replay Win
20th April 1912 vs West Bromwich Albion -
score 1-1 (aet.) (the first game finished 0-0)

First F.A. Cup Final Scorer
H. Tufnell

First League Game & Defeat
1st September 1898 vs Lincoln City - score 0-1

First League Win
10th September 1898 vs Luton Town - score 2-1

First League Scorer
John McArtney

First League Hat-Trick
14th January 1899 vs Small Heath - score 7-2
scored by Jones (3)

First League Draw
5th Nov 1898 vs Manchester City - score 1-1

First League Cup Match & Win
11th October 1960 vs Ipswich Town (a) -
aggregate score 2-0 (1st leg score 2-0)

First League Cup Scorer
Beaumont

First League Cup Defeat
19th October 1960 vs Derby County (a) -
aggregate score 0-3 (1st leg score 0-1)

First League Cup Draw
6th September 1962 vs Hartlepools United (a) -
aggregate score 1-1 (1st leg score 0-1)

First Championship (any Division)
1933-34 3rd Division (North)   Played 42   Pts 62

Probably the first surviving photograph of any Barnsley FC team.

5

BARNSLEY SEASON 1983-84

After two seasons in which they finished in the top half of the Second Division table following their successful Third Division promotion campaign of 1980-1981, Barnsley completed a season of toil and trouble in 14th position.

The campaign started brightly enough with a 3-0 home victory over Fulham on the opening day, but then followed four successive defeats and, after a brief revival of five unbeaten games, there began a constant fight against the growing threat of relegation.

Eventually, a run which brought only one win in ten games - and that at home to bottom team Cambridge United - manager Norman Hunter was sacked following a 3-2 home defeat at the hands of Cardiff City and former Scottish international star Bobby Collins moved up from youth coach to take over as caretaker manager.

The team showed improved form under Collins' guidance and they staved off the relegation threat by taking 12 points out of a possible 15, starting with their biggest win of the season - 5-1 at home to Derby County.

During the season, the club's record transfer fee was smashed when central defender Mick McCarthy joined Manchester City for £200,000 after a total of 272 League appearances for his home-town club.

The leading goalscorer was newcomer David Geddis, with a total of 12, while Ronnie Glavin's tally of 11 meant that he had notched up 92 goals in 205 League and Cup appearances in his five years at the Oakwell Club.

The Reds drew a complete blank in the two major cup competitions, bundled out in the second round of the Milk Cup (having had a bye in the first) by Third Division Walsall, and going down 1-0 away to Sheffield Wednesday in the third round of the F.A. Cup.

Barnsley FC, 1983-84 Season

BARNSLEY SEASON 1984-85

The 1984-85 season began in disastrous fashion with three successive defeats - two of them at home! On the opening day the Reds were pipped 1-0 by Grimsby Town at Blundell Park and then came home losses at the hands of Carlisle United (1-3) and Oldham Athletic (0-1).

Those results appeared to confirm the worst fears of the pessimists, who were prophesying another season of struggle for Bobby Collins, now confirmed as manager after his successful spell as caretaker at the end of the previous campaign, and the Oakwell team.

But then a 2-0 away win at Notts County at Meadow Lane stopped the rot and sparked off an excellent unbeaten League run of 15 matches which completely transformed the situation. Suddenly, far from being a struggling team, the Reds were in the thick of the promotion pack, and by early December they had climbed to third place in the table.

The run came to an end at Oldham on the Sunday before Christmas, a disappointing performance resulting in a 2-1 defeat.

By this time, leading marksman David Geddis had gone to Birmingham City for £80,000 and Roger Wylde and Ron Futcher had arrived in the hope of boosting the Reds' goalscoring output. But it was not to be. The remaining 23 fixtures brought only five wins as Barnsley slipped down the table to finish in 11th position with 58 points.

The highlight of the season was a run to the quarter-finals of the F.A. Cup, which included a 2-1 away victory over First Division Southampton before they were beaten 4-0 at home by European Champions Liverpool in the first match to be televised live from Oakwell.

BARNSLEY SEASON 1985-86

Barnsley opened the 1985-86 season under new management. Allan Clarke, the man who had started the Oakwell Club's revival by leading the Reds out of the Fourth Division at his first attempt in 1979 and then set them firmly on course for Division Two before leaving for Leeds United, returned to the club in the summer, replacing Bobby Collins.

His first game in charge brought a 2-1 defeat at Charlton in a fixture that also saw the League debut of 17-years-old striker David Hirst and the first appearance in a Barnsley shirt of Kenny Burns, signed on a free transfer from Derby County.

By the time the teams met again in mid-December, the Reds were challenging at the top of the table and a 2-1 revenge victory over Charlton lifted them into fourth place.

Hirst was by this time beginning to emerge as a really exciting prospect, his goal in a 1-1 draw at Huddersfield on Boxing Day being his eighth in ten games.

However, the season then turned sour in the space of three days, with home defeats at the hands of Wimbledon and Hull City which sparked off a run of home results which saw the Reds win only once at Oakwell in ten matches. Their away form - they lost only once on their travels in the last seven games - was sufficient to keep them safe from relegation and they eventually finished in a comfortable 12th place with 56 points, one place and two points below the 1984-85 totals.

Newcastle United knocked them out in the second round of the Milk Cup on the away goal rule after they had received a bye in round one, and they crashed out to a 2-0 away defeat at the hands of Third Division Bury in the third round of the F.A. Cup.

Hirst was never quite the same after being injured at Leeds and he finished third in the scoring charts with nine goals behind Ian Walsh (15) and Gordon Owen (11).

BARNSLEY SEASON 1986-87

Remarkably, Barnsley kicked off the 1986-87 campaign without a recognised forward line, David Hirst having been sold to Sheffield Wednesday for £250,000, Gordon Owen to Bristol City for £40,000 and Ian Walsh, the previous season's top scorer, having been given a free transfer to Grimsby Town.

And that certainly had its effect as the Reds crashed to six successive defeats at the start of the season and were left stranded at the bottom of the Second Division after their worst ever start to a campaign.

It began with a 3-2 home defeat at the hands of Crystal Palace, despite scoring the quickest goal of the season when 17-years-old Carl Bradshaw, on loan from Sheffield Wednesday, netted after 38 seconds. Also playing in that game were new signings Steve Lowndes, a Welsh international captured from Millwall for £40,000, and John Beresford, a free transfer recruit from Manchester City.

Grimsby vs Barnsley (Division 2)   27th September 1986

8

A 4-3 away victory over Hull City on New Year's Day, when teenager Ian Chandler scored his first ever hat-trick, was the start of an upturn in fortunes which brought a nine-match unbeaten home run and, despite losing influential defender Larry May to Sheffield Wednesday for a fee of £200,000, the Reds continued to show great character to ensure their Second Division status while at the same time condemning Sunderland to the relegation play-offs with a 3-2 victory at Roker Park in the last game.

The Reds eventually finished in 11th place for the second time in three years, with a total of 55 points.

They also enjoyed good runs in both the Littlewoods and F.A. Cup competitions before bowing out to London giants Spurs and Arsenal respectively. In their first appearance in the Full Members' Cup they were involved in a remarkable game against Sunderland at Roker Park which the home team eventually won 8-7 on penalties, Ian Chandler, making his first appearance for Barnsley against his home-town club, having the decisive 19th spot-kick saved.

BARNSLEY SEASON 1987-88

Early in the season Barnsley were riding high at the top of the Second Division table - the first time they had done so for 41 years - but manager Allan Clarke insisted that his team was not good enough to stay there - and he proved right. The Reds lacked the required consistency and they eventually slipped to a middle-of-the-table placing.

There were, however, several highlights, not least a remarkable 5-2 away victory over First Division West Ham United at Upton Park in the second round of the Littlewoods Cup after the teams had drawn 0-0 at Oakwell. West Ham led 2-0 after half-an-hour, but the Reds fought back to equalise with two goals from Steve Agnew, and three more from John Beresford, Steve Lowndes and John MacDonald completed an amazing comeback.

That brought a home draw with derby rivals Sheffield Wednesday in round three and the season's biggest crowd of 19,343 saw the Reds go down 2-1, former Barnsley striker David Hirst going on as substitute to score the winner for the visitors in the 74th minute.

In the F.A. Cup, a 3-1 home win over Bolton Wanderers was followed by a 2-0 home defeat at the hands of Birmingham City in round four, one of City's goals being scored by Tony Rees, who was later to join the Oakwell Club, and there was a first round exit in the Simod Cup by 2-1 at Chelsea.

Back in the League, the Reds enjoyed a purple patch in October. They staged another big comeback to beat Reading 5-2 after trailing 2-0 with only six minutes gone, and there was another five-goal haul against visitors Stoke City in an identical scoreline, but otherwise Barnsley struggled to find the net, a failing which resulted in the belated transfer deadline signing of David Currie from Darlington for a club record fee of £150,000. He scored twice on his debut against Ipswich at Oakwell but the Reds still lost 3-2.

Barnsley won only one of their last eight games to finish 14th, the season concluding with a 2-2 home draw with West Brom in a game which saw a promising debut for 18-years-old central defender Carl Tiler.

BARNSLEY SEASON 1988-89

Barnsley's eight away win of the season - 3-1 at Walsall - in the final fixture, emphasised the Red worth as promotion contenders as the Oakwell Club came close to achieving their First Division dream.

An end-of-season surge, which saw them beaten only twice in 15 matches, spoke volumes for the character, commitment and ability of a team badly hit by long-term injuries. The club's comparatively small squad was stretched to the limits on occasions, but the players responded magnificently against a backcloth of injury problems, the record £350,000 transfer of John Beresford to Portsmouth, and the continuing lack of revenue through the turnstiles, to finish seventh, only three points away from clinching a promotion play-off place with a club record of 74 Second Division points.

The reds made a good start with an opening unbeaten run of five matches, and at the end of November David Currie, who went on to finish as the club's leading marksman with 20 goals, became the first Barnsley player for 30 years to score four times in a game as the Reds trounced Bournemouth 5-2 at Oakwell.

However, by March a run of five games without a win had sent the Oakwell team sliding to 13th place and play-off hopes were rapidly receding until a 2-1 away win over Bradford City set them off on that strong run which left them only two points behind sixth-from-top Swindon Town.

Skipper Steve Agnew in action against Everton in a 4th Round F.A. Cup-Tie, Feb 1989.
photo courtesy of Barnsley Chronicle

The F.A. Cup again provided memorable matches. In the third round the Reds trounced Second Division leaders Chelsea 4-0 at Oakwell, and then came two thrilling encounters with Stoke City. Over 5,000 fans travelled to the Victoria Ground to see the Reds pegged back to 3-3 with two City goals in the last 13 minutes after the visitors had taken a 3-1 lead, and in the replay three days later, a 70th minute goal by Steve Cooper clinched a passage for the Reds in front of 21,136 fans - Oakwell's biggest gate for six years.

That was comfortably exceeded in the fifth round as 32,551 turned out for the visit of First Division Everton, who edged through courtesy of a Graeme Sharp goal after 15 minutes.

in the Littlewoods Cup the Reds bowed out at the first hurdle to First Division Wimbledon 2-1 on aggregate and they lost to Millwall on a penalty shoot-out at The Den in the first round of the Simod Cup.

BARNSLEY SEASON 1989-90

Through the years Barnsley had earned a reputation for keeping faith with their managers. Angus Seed had spanned the war from 1937 to 1953; Tim Ward was in charge for the following seven years; and Johnny Steele had an 11-year stint from 1960-1971. More recently, Jim Iley was with the club for five years.

However, the 1989-90 season brought the fifth managerial change in the space of 11 years as successive team bosses toiled in vain to build on the double promotion instigated by Allan Clarke. This time it was Clarke himself who was the victim in his second spell with the club.

The previous season the Reds only just missed out on a promotion play-off place, but by November 4, 1989, the team was in deep relegation trouble - 19th in the table - and the former Leeds United and England striker paid the penalty. After a 1-0 home defeat by Portsmouth he was sacked and coach Eric Winstanley was temporarily put in charge.

Winstanley, had a nightmare start to his caretaker reign, the Reds crashing 7-0 to West Brom at The Hawthorns, and he eventually made way for former Manchester City manager Mel Machin. When the latter took over the Reds were third from bottom of the table. In his first four months in charge he led them to the safety of 19th place. His first game on New Year's Day brought a 1-0 victory over Leeds United and remarkably the

Barnsley, 1989-90 Season
photo courtesy of Barnsley Chronicle

11

Reds became the only team to do the double over the eventual Second Division Champions, beating them 2-1 at Elland Road in April.

A run in the F.A. Cup, which took them past Leicester City and Ipswich Town, ended after three games with Sheffield United, and there were early exits in the Littlewoods and Zenith Data Systems Cup competitions.

Machin's early signings included two players from his previous club, Northern Ireland Internationals Gerry Taggart and Gary Fleming.

BARNSLEY SEASON 1990-91

A Brighton goal in the last minute of their final fixture of the season at home to Ipswich Town denied Barnsley a place in the Second Division promotion play-offs.

That Steve Gatting strike inched Brighton into seventh place, leaving the Oakwell team out of the frame in eighth position, despite a spirited 1-0 home victory over Middlesbrough, who were themselves assured of the play-offs by virtue of their superior goal difference.

It was a barren spell during the second half of October and all through November which really cost the Reds their promotion chance. They won only one of 11 fixtures and that left them with a lot to do.

It is to their credit that they got so close. By April they had climbed to seventh in the table only to falter again with a run which brought a draw and three successive defeats and once again lack of consistency had cost them their big chance.

There was disappointment, too, in the major cup competitions. A narrow aggregate victory over Wigan Athletic in the first round of the Rumbelows Cup was followed by a 2-0 aggregate defeat at the hands of Aston Villa, and their F.A. Cup run was even shorter, with a third round defeat at Leeds (0-4) in a replay after a draw at Oakwell.

The Zenith Data Systems Cup did, however, bring some excitement. Ian Banks scored a hat-trick as they beat West Brom 5-3 at the Hawthorns; Sheffield Wednesday were despatched on penalties after a 3-3 draw; and Nottingham Forest were beaten 2-1 at Oakwell before subsequent finalists Everton scored the only goal of the Northern Area semi-final at Barnsley.

At the end of the season central defender Carl Tiler was sold to Nottingham Forest for £1.4 million and skipper Steve Agnew joined Blackburn Rovers for £700,000.

BARNSLEY SEASON 1991-92

With more than £2 million in the coffers as a result of the sale of Carl Tiler and Steve Agnew, Barnsley manager Mel Machin went on a summer spending spree to recruit six new players at a total cost of around £800,000.

They were Gareth Williams (Aston Villa), Lee Butler (Aston Villa), John Pearson (Leeds United), Steve Davis (Burnley), Charlie Bishop (Bury) and Deiniol Graham (Manchester United).

It took the newcomers a while to settle down, however, and the first seven games failed to produce a single victory. After that, it was always a question of fighting for Second Division survival, which was particularly disappointing after going so close to the play-offs the previous season.

The Reds' best period was between December and March, when they lost only three League games, and they eventually finished in a respectable 14th place. Their 1-0 away victory against Grimsby Town in March provided them with their 5,000th League goal.

Once again there were early exits from the major cup competitions - a third round k.o. at the hands of Middlesbrough in the Rumbelows Cup after Blackpool had been overcome on a 2-1 aggregate after extra-time, and a 1-0 defeat on their visit to Norwich City in the third round of the F.A. Cup.

The ZDS Cup again provided a flutter of excitement with a 4-3 extra-time defeat by Leicester City at Filbert Street after fighting back from 3-0 down.

During the season Gerry Taggart won his 11th cap for Northern Ireland, thus breaking the Oakwell Club's record for International appearances previously held by Eddie McMorran, also for Northern Ireland.

There was a record off the field, too, with a profit of £756,391, which beat the previous best of £535,271 and reflected dealings in the transfer market.

The club's transfer record was broken in September when striker David Currie was signed for the second time for a fee of £250,000.

BARNSLEY SEASON 1992-93

Manager Mel Machin's pledge that he would bring promotion in three years return to haunt him during the 1992-93 campaign as the Reds failed to recover fully from another very poor start. It was not until the seventh game of the season that the Reds recorded their first success - a 3-1 away win over Notts County - and after a 2-1 defeat at Leicester on October 3, their record in the League read played nine, won one, drawn two, lost six. As well as struggling in the First Division, they had also made their exit from both the Coca Cola Cup - beaten by Grimsby on penalties - and the Anglo Italian Cup.

However, that game at Filbert Street against Leicester saw the goalscoring debut of striker Wayne Biggins, signed for £200,000 from Stoke City, and his arrival sparked a revival which saw the Reds beaten only twice in the next nine games, which included the biggest win of the season, 5-1 away to Bristol Rovers.

In the new year there was also a good run in the F.A. Cup. A penalty shoot-out victory over Leicester City was followed by an outstanding 4-0 home win over West Ham United, Andy Rammell scoring a hat-trick, before the Reds bowed out 2-0 in the fifth round away to Machin's former club, Manchester City.

Five home games out of seven in March helped the Red continue to make progress in the League, but their outside hopes of a play-off place were dashed in a miserable April which brought only one win, one draw and four defeats, including a 6-0 biggest-of-the-season drubbing away to eventual champions Newcastle United, who earlier in the season had signed Barnsley full-back Mark Robinson for £450,000.

Four days after a 3-1 defeat at Brentford on May 1st, Machin announced that he had decided to relinquish the position of manager and five weeks later Sheffield Wednesday's former England international defender Viv Anderson took over as player-manager, with Hillsborough colleague Danny Wilson accompanying him as player-coach.

1983-84

1	Aug	27	(h)	Fulham	W	3-0	Wilkes 2, Gray	9,851
2	Sep	3	(a)	Manchester C	L	2-3	Chambers, Gray	25,105
3		6	(a)	Portsmouth	L	1-2	Gray	12,804
4		10	(h)	Middlesbrough	L	0-2		10,039
5		17	(a)	Shrewsbury T	L	2-3	Gray, Cunningham	3,867
6		24	(h)	Newcastle U	D	1-1	Cunningham	14,085
7		27	(h)	Grimsby T	W	3-1	Gray, Geddis 2	10,966
8	Oct	1	(a)	Cardiff C	W	3-0	Glavin 2, Geddis	6,433
9		8	(a)	Derby Co	W	2-0	Glavin, Cunningham	12,696
10		15	(h)	Huddersfield T	D	2-2	Geddis, Cunningham	14,096
11		22	(h)	Leeds U	L	0-2		18,236
12		29	(a)	Crystal Palace	W	1-0	May	6,377
13	Nov	5	(a)	Sheffield W	L	0-2		27,491
14		12	(h)	Swansea C	W	3-2	Glavin, Gray 2 (1 pen)	8,161
15		19	(a)	Charlton A	L	2-3	Geddis, Glavin	4,582
16		26	(h)	Brighton & HA	W	3-1	Gray (pen), Airey 2	7,705
17	Dec	3	(a)	Oldham A	L	0-1		5,475
18		10	(h)	Chelsea	D	0-0		10,300
19		17	(a)	Carlisle U	L	2-4	Airey, Joyce	4,812
20		26	(h)	Cambridge U	W	2-0	McGuire, Law	7,486
21		28	(a)	Blackburn R	D	1-1	Glavin	8,954
22		31	(h)	Manchester C	D	1-1	Geddis	17,148
23	Jan	2	(a)	Newcastle U	L	0-1		29,833
24		14	(a)	Fulham	L	0-1		5,085
25	Feb	4	(h)	Cardiff C	L	2-3	McGuire, Geddis	7,107
26		11	(a)	Middlesbrough	L	1-2	Glavin	7,480
27		18	(h)	Crystal Palace	D	1-1	Geddis	6,233
28		25	(a)	Leeds U	W	2-1	Glavin, Johnson	19,138
29	Mar	3	(h)	Sheffield W	L	0-1		20,322
30		10	(a)	Swansea C	L	0-1		4,864
31		13	(h)	Shrewsbury T	W	3-0	Geddis, Glavin, Campbell	5,576
32		17	(h)	Portsmouth	L	0-3		7,030
33		31	(h)	Derby Co	W	5-1	McGuire 2, Plummer, Ronson, Glavin	6,500
34	Apr	7	(a)	Huddersfield T	W	1-0	Geddis	9,657
35		10	(a)	Grimsby T	L	0-1		6,934
36		14	(h)	Charlton A	W	2-0	Glavin, McGuire (pen)	6,321
37		21	(a)	Cambridge U	W	3-0	Geddis 2, Ronson	2,200
38		23	(h)	Blackburn R	D	0-0		7,123
39		28	(a)	Brighton & HA	L	0-1		8,975
40	May	5	(h)	Oldham A	L	0-1		5,539
41		7	(a)	Chelsea	L	1-3	Geddis	29,541
42		12	(h)	Carlisle U	W	2-1	Geddis, Campbell	4,512

FINAL LEAGUE POSITION: 14th in Division Two

Appearances

Sub Appearances

Goals

14

	Horn	Joyce	Chambers	Glavin	Law	McCarthy	Wilkes	Campbell	Ronson	Cunningham	Gray	May	Airey	McGuire	Findlay	Geddis	Rhodes	Fletcher	Whitehouse	Semley	Pickering	Lowe	Johnson	Jeffels	Thomas	Futcher	Plummer	Agnew	
1	1	2	3	4	5	6	7	8	9	10	11																		1
1	1	2	3	4		6	7	8	9	10	11	5																	2
1	1	2	3	4		6	7	8	9	10	11	5																	3
1	1	2	3	4		6	7	8*	9	10	11	5	12																4
1	1	2	3			6	7		9	10	11	5	8	4															5
		2	3	4		6	7			10	11	5	9	8	1														6
		2	3	4		6	7			10	11	5	12	8	1	9*													7
		2	3	4		6	7			10	11	5		8	1	9													8
		2	3	4		6			7	10	11	5		8	1	9													9
		2	3	4		6			7	10	11	5		8	1	9													10
		2	3			6	12	7	4	10	11*	5		8	1	9													11
		4	3	2		6		7		10	11	5		8		9	1												12
		4	3	12	2	6		7*		10	11	5		8		9	1												13
		7	3	4	2	6		11				5	10	8		9	1												14
		7	3	4	2	6		11				5	10	8		9	1												15
		4	3	2		6		11	7			5	10	8		9	1												16
		7	3	4	2*	6	12	11				5	10	8		9	1												17
		2	3	4	12	6		8	7		11*	5	10			9	1												18
		7	3	4		6		8				5	10			9	1	2	11										19
		2	3	4		6		11	8			5	10	7		9	1												20
		2	3	4		6*		11	8			5	10	7		9	1						12						21
		2	3	4				11	8			5	10*	7		9	1						12		6				22
		2	3	4				11	8			5	10*	7		9	1						12		6				23
		4	3	2				11	8			5		7		9	1						12		6	10*			24
		2	3	4		6		11	8			5		7		9	1								10				25
		2*	3	4		6		11	8			5	12	7		10	1								9				26
			3	4	2			11	8			5	9	7		10	1								6				27
			3	4	2			11	8			5	9	7			1								10	6			28
		12	3	4	2			11	8			5		7			1				9*				10	6			29
		2	3	4		6		11	8			5	10	7			1								9				30
		2	3	4		6		11				5	10	7		9	1								8				31
		2	3	4*		6		11	12			5	9	7		10	1								8				32
		2	3	4					7			5	12	8		10	1								9	6	11*		33
		2	3*	4				11	7			5	12	8		9	1								10	6			34
		2	4*	3				11	7			5	12	8		10	1								9	6			35
		2	4	3				11	7			5	9*	8			1					12			10	6			36
		2	4	3				11	7			5	12	8		10*	1								9	6			37
		2	4	3				11	7			5	9*	8			1					12			10	6			38
		2	3	4				11	7			5	9	8		10	1									6			39
		2	3	4				11	7			5		8		10	1								9	6			40
		2	3					11	7			5	4	8		10	1								9	6			41
		2	3					11	7			5		8		10	1						9	4		6			42
5	39	37	34	30	12	10	31	31	13	16	40	20	36	6	31	31	1	1	1	3	2	4	3	13	10	1			
	1		1	1		1		1			7								1	3						1	1		
	1	1	11	1		2	2	2	4	8	1	3	5			14									1			1	

15

1984-85

1	Aug	25	(a)	Grimsby T	L	0-1		6,190
2		27	(h)	Carlisle U	L	1-3	Owen	5,681
3	Sep	1	(h)	Oldham A	L	0-1		5,121
4		4	(a)	Notts Co	W	2-0	May, Plummer	4,703
5		8	(a)	Portsmouth	D	0-0		11,509
6		15	(h)	Cardiff C	W	2-0	Geddis 2 (1 pen)	4,692
7		22	(a)	Huddersfield T	D	1-1	Campbell	6,864
8		29	(h)	Wolverhampton W	W	5-1	Agnew, Geddis 3 (2 pen), Owen	5,566
9	Oct	7	(a)	Crystal Palace	W	1-0	Geddis	6,252
10		13	(h)	Leeds U	W	1-0	Owen	16,199
11		20	(a)	Brighton & HA	D	0-0		10,941
12		27	(h)	Charlton A	W	1-0	Owen	6,301
13	Nov	10	(a)	Middlesbrough	D	0-0		5,227
14		13	(h)	Sheffield U	W	1-0	Thomas	13,468
15		17	(h)	Shrewsbury T	W	3-1	Geddis 2, Plummer (pen)	6,257
16		24	(a)	Birmingham C	D	0-0		9,505
17	Dec	1	(h)	Fulham	W	1-0	Owen	6,742
18		8	(a)	Wimbledon	D	3-3	Geddis 2 (1 pen), Owen	2,871
19		23	(a)	Oldham A	L	1-2	Owen (pen)	5,930
20		26	(a)	Manchester C	D	1-1	Wylde	27,131
21		29	(h)	Notts Co	D	0-0		7,447
22	Jan	1	(h)	Blackburn R	D	1-1	Owen (pen)	10,628
23	Feb	2	(a)	Wolverhampton W	W	1-0	Futcher R	6,864
24		9	(h)	Portsmouth	D	2-2	Campbell, Wylde	7,382
25		23	(a)	Sheffield U	L	1-3	Owen	16,343
26		26	(h)	Middlesbrough	W	1-0	Wylde	6,866
27	Mar	2	(a)	Charlton A	L	3-5	Futcher R 3	3,832
28		13	(h)	Brighton & HA	D	0-0		5,342
29		16	(a)	Leeds U	L	0-2		13,091
30		23	(h)	Crystal Palace	W	3-1	Campbell, Owen 2	4,174
31		30	(a)	Carlisle U	L	0-2		2,784
32	Apr	2	(h)	Oxford U	W	3-0	Owen 3	6,029
33		6	(h)	Manchester C	D	0-0		12,930
34		8	(a)	Blackburn R	D	0-0		9,320
35		13	(h)	Huddersfield T	W	2-1	Futcher R, Wylde (pen)	7,832
36		20	(a)	Shrewsbury T	L	0-2		3,171
37		23	(a)	Cardiff C	L	0-3		3,044
38		27	(h)	Birmingham C	L	0-1		6,757
39		30	(h)	Grimsby T	D	0-0		3,261
40	May	4	(a)	Fulham	D	1-1	Plummer	3,721
41		6	(h)	Wimbledon	D	0-0		3,053
42		11	(a)	Oxford U	L	0-4		13,196

FINAL LEAGUE POSITION: 11th in Division Two

Appearances

Sub Appearances

Goals

Rhodes	Joyce	Chambers	Ronson	May	Futcher P	Owen	Thomas	Walsh	Geddis	Campbell	Plummer	Law	Agnew	Baker	McGuire	Jeffels	Cross	Wylde	Futcher R	Goodison	Gray	No.
1	2	3	4	5	6	7	8	9	10	11	12											1
1	2	3	4	5	6	7	8	9	10		11											2
1	2		4	5	6	7	8		10*	11	9	3	12									3
	2		4	5	6	7	8	9		11	10	3		1								4
	2		4	5	6		8	9	7	11	10*	3		1	12							5
	2		4	5	6		8	9	7	11	10	3		1	12							6
	2		4	5*	6		8	12	10	11	9	3		1	7							7
	2		4		6	7	8	12	10	11		3	9*	1		5						8
	2		4		6		8	12	10	7		3	9*	1		5	11					9
	2		4		6	7	8	9	10*	11	12	3		1		5						10
	2		4		6	7	8	9		11	10	3		1		5						11
	2		4		6	7	8			11	10	3	9	1		5						12
	2		4		6	7	8		10	11	9	3		1		5						13
	2		4		6	7	8		10	11	9	3		1		5						14
	2		4		6	7	8		10	11	9	3		1		5						15
	2		4		6	7	8		10*	11	9	3		1	12	5						16
	2		4		6	7	8	9		11	10	3		1		5						17
	2		4		6	7	8		10	11		3		1		5		9				18
	2		4		6	7	8			11	12	3		1		5		10	9			19
	2		4	5	6		8	9		11	7	3		1				10				20
	2		4	5	6	7	8	12		11	9	3		1				10*				21
	2		4	5	6	7	8	9		11	10	3		1								22
	2	3	4			7	8			11	12	5		1				10	9*	6		23
	2		4		6	7	8			11		3		1				10	9	5		24
	2		4		6	7	8			11		3		1				9	10	5		25
	2		4			7	8			11		3		1	6			10	9	5		26
	2		4		6	7	8			11		3	10	1		5		9				27
	2		4	5	6	7	8			11		3		1				9	3	10		28
	2		4	5	6	7	8	9		11		3	10*	1				12				29
1	2		4	5	6	7	8			11		3	9					10				30
1	2		4	5	6	7	8			11		3						10	9			31
	2		4	5	6	7	8			11		3	12	1				10	9*			32
		3	4	5	6	7	8			11				1				10	9	2		33
	2	3	4	5	6	7				11				1				10	9	8		34
	2	3		5	6					11			7	1				10	9	8	4	35
	2		4	5	6	7	8			11		3		1				10*	9	12		36
	2			5	6	7	8	9*				3		1				10	12	4	11	37
	2		4	5	6	7	8			11	10*	3		1				12	9			38
	2		4	5		7	8			11		3	10*	1	6			9		12		39
	2	3	4			7	8		10	11		5		1	6			9				40
	2		4			7	8		10	11		5*		1	6			9	12	3		41
	2		4	5		7	8	10		11				1	6*			9	12	3		42
5	41	7	40	23	36	36	40	12	14	38	22	35	8	37	1	18	1	16	18	9	5	
						4			4		2		3				1	1		3	2	
		1		14	1			10	3	3		1						4	5			

17

1985-86

1	Aug	17	(a)	Charlton A	L	1-2	Gray (pen)	4,178
2		20	(h)	Brighton & HA	W	3-2	Thoams 2, Walsh	5,051
3		24	(h)	Stoke C	D	0-0		6,598
4		26	(a)	Norwich C	D	1-1	Owen	13,510
5		31	(h)	Fulham	W	2-0	Owen, Walsh	5,197
6	Sep	3	(a)	Wimbledon	L	0-1		2,351
7		7	(a)	Carlisle U	D	1-1	Owen (pen)	2,418
8		14	(h)	Shrewsbury T	W	2-0	Campbell, Walsh	4,516
9		21	(h)	Grimsby T	W	1-0	Walsh	5,365
10		28	(a)	Middlesbrough	D	0-0		5,589
11	Oct	5	(h)	Portsmouth	L	0-1		7,064
12		12	(a)	Bradford C	L	0-2		5,707
13		19	(a)	Sheffield U	L	1-3	Owen (pen)	11,167
14		27	(h)	Leeds U	W	3-0	Owen, Hirst, Walsh	8,302
15	Nov	2	(h)	Oldham A	W	1-0	Donachie (og)	7,118
16		9	(a)	Blackburn R	W	3-0	Hirst 2, Walsh	5,927
17		16	(h)	Sunderland	D	1-1	Hirst	9,410
18		23	(a)	Crystal Palace	L	0-1		5,625
19		30	(h)	Millwall	W	2-1	Owen (pen), Gray	4,340
20	Dec	7	(a)	Brighton & HA	W	1-0	Hirst	8,819
21		14	(h)	Charlton A	W	2-1	Hirst 2	6,231
22		21	(a)	Stoke C	D	0-0		9,856
23		26	(a)	Huddersfield T	D	1-1	Hirst	10,575
24		28	(h)	Wimbledon	L	0-1		8,949
25	Jan	1	(h)	Hull C	L	1-4	Owen (pen)	8,363
26		11	(a)	Shrewsbury T	L	0-3		2,756
27		18	(a)	Fulham	L	0-2		3,580
28	Feb	1	(h)	Norwich C	D	2-2	Hirst, Thomas	5,608
29		15	(a)	Leeds U	W	2-0	Walsh 2	11,765
30	Mar	8	(a)	Portsmouth	D	1-1	Walsh	10,426
31		15	(h)	Bradford C	D	2-2	Thomas, Owen (pen)	7,512
32		22	(h)	Carlisle U	L	1-2	Walsh	4,400
33		25	(h)	Middlesbrough	D	0-0		3,827
34		29	(a)	Hull C	W	1-0	Plummer	7,903
35		31	(h)	Huddersfield T	L	1-3	Plummer	5,746
36	Apr	6	(a)	Oldham A	D	1-1	Thomas	3,971
37		8	(h)	Sheffield U	W	2-1	Walsh 2	5,451
38		12	(h)	Blackburn R	D	1-1	Walsh	4,256
39		19	(a)	Sunderland	L	0-2		12,349
40		22	(a)	Grimsby T	W	2-1	Walsh, Owen	4,009
41		26	(h)	Crystal Palace	L	2-4	Owen, Walsh	3,862
42	May	3	(a)	Millwall	D	2-2	Plummer, Owen (pen)	4,230

FINAL LEAGUE POSITION: 12th in Division Two

Appearances

Sub Appearances

Goals

Baker	Joyce	Law	Thomas	Burns	Jeffels	Goodison	Hirst	Walsh	Gray	Campbell	Ronson	Futcher	Glavin	Owen	Plummer	May	Cross	Agnew	Ogley	McKenzie	Jonsson	Aylott	Kiwomya	#
1	2	3*	4	5	6	7	8	9	10	11	12													1
1	2		4	5	7	3	8	9	10*	11		6	12											2
1	2		4	5	10	3	8	9*		11		6		7	12									3
1	2		8	5	10	3		9		11		6	4	7										4
1	2			5	8*	3	12	9	10	11		6	4	7										5
1	2			5	8	3		9	10	11		6	4	7										6
1	2			5		3		9	10	11		6	4*	7	12	8								7
1	2		8	5				9	3	11		6		7		4	10							8
1	2		8	5				9	3	11		6		7		4	10							9
1	2		8	5				9	3	11		6		7		4	10							10
1	2		8	5			7	9	3	11		6				4	10							11
1	2		10	5			8*		3	11		6	4		12	7		9						12
1	2		10	5					3	11	8	6				7	4	9						13
1	2		8			4	10	9	3			6		7		11	5							14
1	2		8			4	10	9	3			6		7		11	5							15
1	2		8			4	10	9	3			6		7		11	5							16
1	2		8			4	10	9	3			6		7		11	5							17
1	2		8	12		4	10	9	3			6			7*		5		11					18
1	2		8			4	10	9	3	11		6		7			5							19
1	2		8			4	10	3	9			6		7		11	5							20
1	2		8			4	10	9	3			6		7		11	5							21
1	2		8			4	10	9	3			6		7		11	5							22
1	2		8			4	10	9	3			6		7		11	5							23
1	2		8	12		4	10	9	3			6		7		11*	5							24
1	2		8	9		4	10		3			6		7		11	5							25
1	2		8				10	9	3	11		6		7			5			4				26
1	2		8	12				9*	3	11		6		7	10	5	4							27
1			4	2			10	9	3			6		7		5	11				8			28
1			4	2			10*	9	3	12		6		7		5	11				8			29
1	2		4					9	3			6		7		5	11				8	10		30
1	2		4					9	3			6		7*	12	5	11				8	10		31
1	2		4					9	3			6		7	12	5	11*				8	10		32
1	2		4				10	8	3			6		7		5	11					9		33
1	2		4		6		10		3	11				7		5	8					9		34
1	2		4			3	10			11		6		7		5	8					9		35
1	2		4				8	12	10	11*		6		7		5	3					9		36
1	2		4				8		10	11		6		7		5	3					9		37
1	2		4	12			8		10	11		6		7		5	3					9*		38
1	2		4				9	10	8	11		6		7		5	3							39
1	2		4		6*		12	9	8	10				7		5	3						11	40
1	2		4	12	6		11	9	8	10*				7		5	3							41
1	2		4					9	8	11		6		7	10	5	3							42
42	40	1	39	19	10	19	26	33	36	28	1	37	5	32	18	36	20	2	2	1	5	9	1	
				3	1	2	2			1	1		1		5									
		5					9	15	2	1			11	3										

19

1986-87

#	Month	Date	H/A	Opponent	Result	Score	Scorers	Attendance
1	Aug	23	(h)	Crystal Palace	L	2-3	Bradshaw, Thomas	4,629
2		25	(a)	Oldham A	L	0-2		5,326
3		30	(a)	Millwall	L	0-1		4,001
4	Sep	2	(h)	Leeds U	L	0-1		6,839
5		6	(h)	Portsmouth	L	0-2		4,341
6		13	(a)	Shrewsbury T	L	0-1		2,435
7		20	(h)	Plymouth A	D	1-1	May	4,163
8		27	(a)	Grimsby T	W	1-0	Gray	4,789
9	Oct	4	(a)	Birmingham C	D	1-1	Foreman	6,427
10		11	(h)	Bradford C	W	2-0	Gray 2 (1 pen)	6,884
11		18	(a)	Brighton & HA	D	1-1	Dobbin	7,923
12		25	(h)	Sheffield U	D	2-2	Gray 2 (1 pen)	7,519
13	Nov	1	(h)	Blackburn R	D	1-1	Gray (pen)	4,861
14		8	(a)	Reading	D	0-0		5,346
15		15	(h)	Derby Co	L	0-1		8,283
16		22	(a)	Ipswich T	L	0-1		10,150
17		29	(h)	West Brom A	D	2-2	Lowndes, Beresford	5,750
18	Dec	13	(h)	Sunderland	W	1-0	Gray	5,535
19		20	(a)	Portsmouth	L	1-2	Ferry	9,568
20		26	(h)	Stoke C	L	0-2		7,436
21		27	(a)	Derby Co	L	2-3	Chandler, Gray	17,574
22	Jan	1	(a)	Hull C	W	4-3	Chandler 3, Duggan	4,879
23		3	(h)	Oldham A	D	1-1	MacDonald	8,101
24		24	(a)	Crystal Palace	W	1-0	MacDonald	6,011
25	Feb	7	(h)	Millwall	W	1-0	Dobbin	5,461
26		14	(a)	Leeds U	D	2-2	Sheridan (og), Dobbin	14,216
27		24	(h)	Grimsby T	W	1-0	MacDonald	5,136
28		28	(a)	Plymouth A	L	0-2		9,588
29	Mar	3	(h)	Shrewsbury T	W	2-1	MacDonald, Gray	4,718
30		7	(a)	Sheffield U	L	0-1		8,971
31		14	(h)	Brighton & HA	W	3-1	MacDonald, Wylde, Gray	4,733
32		21	(a)	Bradford C	D	0-0		9,648
33		28	(h)	Birmingham C	D	2-2	Wylde 2	4,688
34		31	(a)	Huddersfield T	D	2-2	MacDonald, Thomas	7,569
35	Apr	4	(h)	Reading	W	2-0	Wylde, Gray	4,285
36		11	(a)	Blackburn R	L	2-4	Clarke, MacDonald	7,320
37		18	(h)	Hull C	D	1-1	Wylde	5,607
38		20	(a)	Stoke C	W	2-1	Thomas, Clarke	7,263
39		25	(h)	Ipswich T	W	2-1	Thomas, Wylde	5,536
40	May	2	(a)	West Brom A	W	1-0	Clarke	6,361
41		4	(h)	Huddersfield T	L	0-1		8,564
42		9	(a)	Sunderland	W	3-2	Dobbin, Wylde, Thomas	19,059

FINAL LEAGUE POSITION: 11th in Division Two

Appearances

Sub Appearances

Goals

20

Baker	Joyce	Cross	Thomas	May	Futcher	Lowndes	Bradshaw	Campbell	Gray	Beresford	Plummer	Wylde	Ogley	Agnew	Chandler	Foreman	Dobbin	Malcolm	Hedworth	Duggan	Ferry	Clarke	MacDonald	Jeffels	#
1	2	3	4	5	6	7	8	9	10	11															1
1	2	3	4	5	6	7	8	9*	10	11	12														2
1	2	3	4	5	6	7	8*	12	10	11			9												3
1	2	3	4	5	6	7	8	12	10	11			9*												4
1	2	3	4		6	7	8*		10	11	12		5	9											5
1	2	3	4		6	7*	8		10		12		5	11	9										6
1	2		4	5	6	7			3		12			11	9*	8	10								7
1	2	3	4	5	6				10	7				11	9	8									8
1	2	3	4	5	6				10	7				11	12	9*	8								9
	2		4	5		7			3	10			6	11	12	9*	8	1							10
	2		4	5		7			3	10			6	11		9	8	1							11
	2		4	5		7*			10				6	11	12	9	8	1	3						12
1	2		4	5		7			10				6	11*	12	9	8		3						13
1	2		4	5	6	7			10					12	11	9	8		3*						14
1	2		4	5	6	7*			10					12	11	9	8		3						15
1		3	4	5		7			10	11		2			9	8*					6	12			16
1		3	4	5		7*			6	11	8	2			9							12	10		17
1			4	5	6				3	11		2			7		9				8		10		18
1			4	5	6				3	11		2	8		7		9						10		19
1		3	4	5	6				11			2			7	8			12	9*			10		20
1			4	5	6				3			2			7	9			8			11	10		21
1		3	4	5	6				7			2	8				9					11	10		22
1		3	4	5	6				7			2	8				9					11	10		23
1	2	3	4	5	6				7				8		9				12			11	10*		24
1	2	3	4	5	6				7*				8		9				12			11	10		25
1	2	3	4		6				5				8		9	7						11	10		26
1	2	3	4		6				5				8		9	7						11	10		27
1	2	3			6				5	12		4	8		9	7						11*	10		28
1	2				6				5	12		4	8		7*		9		3			11	10		29
1	2		4		6				5			7	8				9		3			11	10		30
1	2		4		6				5	3		7	8				9					11	10		31
1	2		4		6				5	3		7	8				9					11	10		32
1	2		4		6				5	3		7	8				9		12			11*	10		33
1	2		4		6				5	3		7	8				9					11	10		34
1	2		4		6				5	3		7	8				9					11	10		35
1	2		4		6				5	3		7	8*				9		12			11	10		36
1	2		4		6				5			7	8				9		3			11	10		37
1	2		4		6				5			7	8				9		3			11	10		38
1	2		4		6				5			7	8				9		3*			11	10		39
1	2		4		6								8			7	9		3			11	10	5	40
1	2		4		6				10				8		7	12	9		3*			11	5		41
1	2		4		6				5	3		7	8*				9					11	10	12	42
39	34	18	40	22	36	15	6	2	40	23		15	17	31	8	15	30	3	15	1	3	22	25	2	
								2		4	3		2	4	1		5	1	1		1	1	1		
		5	1		1	1		11	1			7		4	1	4			1	1	3	7			

1987-88

1	Aug	16	(h)	Leeds U	D	1-1	Wylde	9,778
2		18	(a)	Blackburn R	W	1-0	MacDonald	6,708
3		22	(a)	Millwall	L	1-3	Lowndes	6,017
4		29	(h)	Crystal Palace	W	2-1	Wylde, MacDonald	4,853
5		31	(a)	Bournemouth	W	2-1	MacDonald, Lowndes	7,480
6	Sep	5	(h)	Plymouth A	W	2-1	Wylde 2 (1 pen)	6,976
7		12	(a)	Aston Villa	D	0-0		12,621
8		15	(h)	Swindon T	L	0-1		7,773
9		26	(a)	Oldham A	L	0-1		5,853
10		29	(h)	Sheffield U	L	1-2	Agnew	10,203
11	Oct	3	(a)	Ipswich T	L	0-1		10,992
12		10	(a)	Leicester C	D	0-0		8,669
13		17	(h)	Hull C	L	1-3	Lowndes	7,310
14		20	(h)	Reading	W	5-2	MacDonald 2, Wylde, Joyce, Richardson (og)	4,396
15		24	(a)	Manchester C	D	1-1	Thomas	17,063
16		31	(h)	Stoke C	W	5-2	MacDonald, Wylde 2, Dobbin, Lowndes	5,908
17	Nov	3	(a)	Birmingham C	L	0-2		6,622
18		7	(h)	Bradford C	W	3-0	Gray, Lowndes, Wylde	11,569
19		14	(a)	Huddersfield T	D	2-2	MacDonald, Gray	8,629
20		21	(h)	Shrewsbury T	W	2-1	Lowndes, Thomas	5,364
21		28	(a)	Middlesbrough	L	0-2		12,732
22	Dec	5	(h)	West Brom A	W	3-1	Agnew 2, Foreman	5,395
23		19	(h)	Millwall	W	4-1	Agnew 2 (1 pen), McGugan, Broddle	5,011
24		26	(h)	Oldham A	D	1-1	Thomas	8,676
25	Jan	1	(a)	Crystal Palace	L	2-3	Agnew, Lowndes	8,563
26		2	(h)	Aston Villa	L	1-3	Foreman	11,562
27		16	(a)	Leeds U	W	2-0	Foreman 2	19,028
28	Feb	13	(h)	Blackburn R	L	0-1		8,972
29		20	(a)	Sheffield U	L	0-1		11,861
30		27	(h)	Ipswich T	L	2-3	Currie 2	6,482
31	Mar	5	(a)	Hull C	W	2-1	Dobbin, Beresford	7,622
32		8	(h)	Bournemouth	W	2-1	Beresford, Lowndes	6,140
33		12	(h)	Leicester C	D	1-1	Rees	7,447
34		15	(a)	Swindon T	L	0-3		7,558
35		19	(a)	Stoke C	L	1-3	Rees	8,029
36		26	(h)	Manchester C	W	3-1	Joyce, Beresford, Hinchcliffe (og)	9,061
37	Apr	2	(a)	Bradford C	D	1-1	Thomas	15,098
38		4	(h)	Huddersfield T	W	1-0	Currie	7,590
39		9	(a)	Reading	L	1-2	Hicks (og)	4,849
40		15	(a)	Plymouth A	D	0-0		8,059
41		23	(h)	Birmingham C	D	2-2	Currie 2	4,949
42		30	(a)	Shrewsbury T	D	1-1	Lowndes	4,712
43	May	2	(h)	Middlesbrough	L	0-3		13,240
44		7	(a)	West Brom A	D	2-2	Currie 2	8,483

FINAL LEAGUE POSITION: 14th in Division Two

Appearances

Sub Appearances

Goals

Baker	Joyce	Beresford	Thomas	Gray	Futcher	Wylde	Agnew	Dobbin	MacDonald	Clarke	Lowndes	Jeffels	Cross	Robinson	Broddle	McGugan	Foreman	Coatsworth	Hedworth	Currie	Rees	Blair	Rolph	Tiler	#
1	2	3	4	5	6	7	8	9*	10	11	12														1
1	2		4	5	6	7	8		10	11*	9		3	12											2
1	2		4	5	6	7	8		10	11*	9		3		12										3
1	2	3*	4	5	6	7	8		10	11†	9			12	14										4
1	2	3	4	5	6	7	8		10	11	9														5
1	2		4	5	6	7	8		10	11	9		3												6
1	2	12	4	5	6	7	8		10	11*	9		3												7
1	2		4	5	6	7	8		10	11	9		3												8
1	2	12	4	5	6	7	8		10†	11*	9		3		14										9
1	2	12	4	5	6	7	8		10	11†	9		3*		14										10
1	2	12	4	5	6	7*	8		10		9		3		11										11
1	2	7	4	5	6		8		10		9		3		11										12
1	2	7	4	5	6		8	14	10†		9		3		11*	12									13
1	2	11	4	5	6	7	8		10		9		3												14
1	2	11*	4	5	6	7	8	12	10		9		3												15
1	2		4	11	6	7	8		10*		9		3		12	5									16
1	2		4	11	6	7†	8		10*		9		3		14	5	12								17
1	2		4	11	6	7	8		10		9		3			5									18
1	2		4	11	6	7	8		10		9		3			5									19
1	2	11	4	5	6	7	8		10		9		3												20
1	2	11	4		6	7	8		10		9		3			5									21
1	2	11	4		6		8		10		9		3*		12	5				7					22
1			4		6		8		10*	12	9		3		11	5	7	2							23
1	10*		4	14	6		8			12	9		3		11	5	7†	2							24
1	10		4		6		8				9		3		11	5	7	2							25
1	10		4		6		8				9		3		11	5	7	2							26
1	2	12	4		6		8*	10			9		3		11	5	7								27
1	2	11	4		6	7	8		10*		9		3		12	5									28
1	2	11†	4		6		8*	4		12	9		3		10	5	7								29
1	2	11	4		6		8*	10			9		3		12	5				7					30
1			4		6		8		10		9	12	3			5			2*	7	11				31
1			4		6		8		10*		9	2	3		12	5				7	11				32
1	2	4†	14		6		8		10*		9		3		12	5				7	11				33
1	2		4		6		8		10*		9		3		12	5				7	11				34
1	2	10	4		6						9		3			5				7	11	8			35
1	2	10	4		6						9		3			5				7	11	8			36
1	2	10*	4		6						9		3			5			12	7	11	8			37
1	2	10*	4		6						9		3			5			12	7	11	8			38
1	2	10	4		6						9		3			5			12	7	11	8*			39
1	2	10	4								9	6	3			5			12	7	11*	8			40
1	2	10*	4				8	12			9	6	3			5				7	11				41
1	2	3	4		6				10	11*	9					5	8†			7	12		14		42
1	2	3	4		6				10*	11	9				14	5	8†			7	12				43
1	2	10	4					9	6*		8					5				7	11	3	12		44
44	38	29	40	20	41	19	25	14	31	12	43	6	36	1	9	28	7	3	4	15	12	6	1		
5	2		1		2	2	2		1	1	2	2	10	1	2	3	1			2		1	1		
2	3	4	2		8	6	2	7					9		1	1	4			7	2				

23

1988-89

1	Aug	27	(a)	Oldham A	D	1-1	Cooper	6,551
2		29	(h)	Swindon T	D	1-1	Lowndes	6,034
3	Sep	3	(h)	Stoke C	W	1-0	Agnew	5,682
4		10	(a)	Hull C	D	0-0		5,654
5		17	(h)	Chelsea	D	1-1	Dobbin	6,942
6		21	(a)	Leeds U	L	0-2		17,390
7		24	(h)	Manchester C	L	1-2	Shotton	9,300
8	Oct	1	(a)	Birmingham C	W	5-3	Beresford, Broddle, Currie, Rees, Lowndes	4,892
9		5	(a)	Brighton & HA	W	1-0	Currie (pen)	7,327
10		8	(h)	West Brom A	W	2-1	Currie, Thomas	5,674
11		15	(a)	Blackburn R	L	1-2	Mail (og)	9,316
12		22	(h)	Ipswich T	W	2-0	Cooper 2	6,325
13		25	(a)	Watford	L	0-4		10,356
14		29	(h)	Plymouth A	W	3-1	Cooper, Thomas, Dobbin	5,485
15	Nov	5	(a)	Crystal Palace	D	1-1	Broddle	7,768
16		12	(h)	Bradford C	D	0-0		8,838
17		19	(a)	Portsmouth	L	0-3		10,001
18		26	(h)	Bournemouth	W	5-2	Currie 4 (1 pen), Dobbin	4,937
19	Dec	3	(a)	Oxford U	L	0-2		4,449
20		10	(h)	Walsall	W	1-0	Broddle ·	5,173
21		17	(h)	Leicester C	W	3-0	Currie (pen), McGugan, Agnew	6,477
22		26	(a)	Sunderland	L	0-1		21,994
23		31	(a)	Shrewsbury T	W	3-2	Currie (pen), Lowndes, Moyes (og)	4,401
24	Jan	2	(h)	Hull C	L	0-2		9,879
25		14	(a)	Swindon T	D	0-0		10,201
26		21	(h)	Oldham A	W	4-3	Lowndes, Skipper (og), Currie 2 (1 pen)	7,879
27	Feb	4	(h)	Brighton & HA	D	2-2	Cooper, Agnew	12,498
28		11	(a)	West Brom A	D	1-1	Lowndes	12,650
29		21	(a)	Ipswich T	L	0-2		9,995
30		25	(h)	Blackburn R	L	0-1		8,777
31		28	(h)	Watford	D	2-2	MacDonald, Shotton	6,163
32	Mar	4	(a)	Bradford C	W	2-1	Currie (pen), MacDonald	11,085
33		11	(h)	Crystal Palace	D	1-1	MacDonald	7,055
34		19	(h)	Leeds U	D	2-2	Agnew, Robinson	11,578
35		25	(a)	Stoke C	D	1-1	Currie (pen)	10,209
36		27	(h)	Sunderland	W	3-0	Robinson, Cooper, Dobbin (pen)	8,070
37	Apr	1	(a)	Chelsea	L	3-5	McLaughlin (og), Dobbin, Agnew	16,023
38		8	(h)	Shrewsbury T	W	1-0	MacDonald	5,252
39		11	(a)	Leicester C	W	1-0	Lowndes	7,266
40		15	(h)	Birmingham C	D	0-0		6,464
41		22	(a)	Manchester C	W	2-1	Cooper (og), Shotton	21,274
42		25	(a)	Plymouth A	W	2-1	Currie, Shotton	5,468
43		29	(a)	Bournemouth	L	2-3	O'Driscoll (og), Shotton	5,520
44	May	1	(h)	Oxford U	W	1-0	Evans (og)	5,940
45		6	(h)	Portsmouth	W	1-0	Currie (pen)	5,178
46		13	(a)	Walsall	W	3-1	MacDonald, Currie, Agnew	3,966

FINAL LEAGUE POSITION: 7th in Division Two

Appearances

Sub Appearances

Goals

24

Baker	Joyce	Beresford	Dobbin	McGugan	Futcher	Lowndes	Agnew	Cooper	Currie	Thomas	MacDonald	Clarke	Broddle	Shotton	Foreman	Marshall	Rees	Robinson	Tiler	No.
1	2	3	4	5	6	7*	8	9	10	11	12									1
1	2	3	4	5	6	7	8	9	10	11										2
1	2	3*	5		6	7	8	9	10	4	12	11†	14							3
1	2	3	11		6	7	8	9	10	4				5						4
1	2	3	11		6	7	8	9		4	10*			5	12					5
1	2	3	11		6	7	8	9	10	4				5						6
1	2	3	11		6	7*	8	9	10	4				5	12					7
1	2	3	12		6	7	8*		10	4			11	5			9			8
1	2	3			6	7	8	12	10	4			11	5			9*			9
1	2	3	14	6†		7*	8	12	10	4			11	5			9			10
1	2	3	14		6	7†	8*	12	10	4			11	5			9			11
1	2	3	8		6	12	14	9	10*	4			11	5			7†			12
1	2	3	8		6	7*	12	9		4			11	5			10			13
1	2	3	8		6			9		4	10		11	5			7			14
1	2	3*	8	12	6			9		4	10		11	5			7			15
1	2		8	3	6			9	10*	4	12		11	5			7			16
1	2		8	3	6	9			10	4			11	5			7			17
1	2		8	3	6				10	4	7		11	5			9*	12		18
1	2		8	3	6	12	14		10	4	7*		11	5			9†			19
1	2	3	8	5*	6		12	9	10	4			11				7†	14		20
1	2	3		5	6	7	8	9	10	4			11							21
1	2	3	12	5	6	7	8*	9†	10	4			11				14			22
1	2	8		5	6	7		9	10	4	12		11	3*						23
1	2	3	12	5	6			9	10	4	8		11				7*			24
1	2	3	8	5	6	7		9	10		11		4							25
1	2	3*	4	5	6	7	8	9	10		11		12							26
1	2	3		5*	6		8	9	10		11	12	4				7			27
1	2	3		5	6	7	8	9			11		10	4						28
1	2	3	4	5*	6	7†	8	9	10		11		14	12						29
1	2	3	4		6		8	9	10	11*	12			5			7			30
1	2		4		6		8		10	11	3		9	5			7			31
1	2	3	4		6		8		10	11			9	5			7			32
1	2		4		6		8		10	11	3*		9	5	12		7			33
1	2		4		6	9	8	10*		11	3				12		7	5		34
1	2		4		6	9	8	12	10	11	3						7*	5		35
1	2		4		6	9	8	12	10*	11	3			5			7			36
1	2		4		6	9	8	12	10	11†	3			5	14		7*			37
1	2				6	8	9*		10	11	3			5						38
1	2		4		6	7	8	9	10	11	3			5						39
1	2		4		6	7	8	9	10*	11	3			5			12			40
1	2		4		6	9	8		10	11	3			5			7			41
1	2		4		6	9	8		10	11	3			5			7			42
1	2		4		6	9	8	12	10	11	3			5			7*			43
1	2		4			8	9	10*		11	3			5	12		7	6		44
1	2		4		6	12	8	9*	10	11	3			5			7			45
1			4		6	9	8		10	11	3			5			7	2		46
46	45	27	36	19	41	30	35	28	41	24	28	3	34	35			15	15	4	
			5	1		3	4	7		4		4	2	5	1	2	3			
		1	5	1		6	6	6	16	2	5	3	5			1	2			

25

1989-90

1	Aug	19	(a)	Ipswich T	L	1-3	Lowndes	12,100
2		26	(h)	Brighton & HA	W	1-0	Currie	5,920
3	Sep	2	(a)	Plymouth A	L	1-2	MacDonald	7,708
4		5	(h)	Stoke C	W	3-2	Agnew, Cooper, Lowndes	8,584
5		9	(h)	Middlesbrough	D	1-1	Shotton	10,535
6		16	(a)	Swindon T	D	0-0		6,540
7		23	(h)	Bradford C	W	2-0	Agnew, Foreman	8,992
8		26	(h)	Wolverhampton W	D	2-2	Currie 2	10,161
9		30	(a)	Blackburn R	L	0-5		8,415
10	Oct	7	(a)	Oldham A	L	0-2		6,769
11		14	(h)	Port Vale	L	0-3		6,475
12		17	(h)	Sheffield U	L	1-2	Agnew	16,629
13		21	(a)	Oxford U	W	3-2	Banks 2, Foreman	3,863
14		28	(h)	Leicester C	D	2-2	Archdeacon, Currie (pen)	6,856
15		31	(a)	Sunderland	L	2-4	Currie, Tiler	14,234
16	Nov	4	(h)	Portsmouth	L	0-1		5,524
17		11	(a)	West Brom A	L	0-7		9,317
18		18	(h)	Newcastle U	D	1-1	Currie	10,475
19		25	(a)	Hull C	W	2-1	Cooper, Currie	5,715
20	Dec	2	(h)	Ipswich T	L	0-1		6,097
21		9	(a)	Stoke C	W	1-0	Cooper	10,163
22		16	(a)	Bournemouth	L	1-2	Lowndes	5,506
23		26	(h)	Watford	L	0-1		7,357
24		30	(h)	Leeds U	W	1-0	Foreman	14,841
25	Jan	1	(a)	West Ham U	L	2-4	Dobbin, Archdeacon	18,391
26		13	(a)	Brighton & HA	D	1-1	Taggart	6,856
27		20	(h)	Plymouth A	D	1-1	Smith	7,224
28	Feb	3	(a)	Bradford C	D	0-0		9,923
29		10	(h)	Swindon T	L	0-1		7,179
30		224	(h)	Hull C	D	1-1	Cooper	8,901
31	Mar	3	(a)	Newcastle U	L	1-4	Agnew	18,998
32		10	(a)	Wolverhampton W	D	1-1	Agnew (pen)	15,995
33		17	(h)	Oldham A	W	1-0	Milligan (og)	10,598
34		19	(a)	Port Vale	L	1-2	Banks	7,036
35		24	(a)	Sheffield U	W	2-1	Agnew, Saville	15,951
36		31	(h)	Oxford U	W	1-0	Smith	7,096
37	Apr	3	(h)	Blackburn R	D	0-0		8,713
38		7	(a)	Leicester C	D	2-2	Cooper, Agnew	8,620
39		10	(h)	Sunderland	W	1-0	McCord	11,141
40		14	(h)	West Ham U	D	1-1	Taggart	10,344
41		17	(a)	Watford	D	2-2	Lowndes, Agnew (pen)	7,289
42		21	(h)	Bournemouth	L	0-1		7,415
43		25	(a)	Leeds U	W	2-1	O'Connell, Archdeacon	31,700
44		28	(h)	West Brom A	D	2-2	O'Connell, Saville	10,334
45	May	2	(a)	Middlesbrough	W	1-0	Smith	17,015
46		5	(a)	Portsmouth	L	1-2	Saville	8,415

FINAL LEAGUE POSITION: 19th in Division Two

Appearances

Sub Appearances

Goals

Baker	Tiler	Broddle	Dobbin	Shotton	Futcher	Lowndes	Agnew	Cooper	Currie	Robinson	MacDonald	Banks	Wardle	Foreman	Archdeacon	Cross	Dunphy	Smith	McCord	Marshall	Taggart	Glover	Gray	Thomas	Saville	Fleming	O'Connell	No.
1	2	3	4	5	6	7	8	9	10	11																		1
1	2	3	4	5†	6	7	8	9*	10	11	12	14																2
1		3	4	2	6	7	8	12	10	11	9*	5																3
1	12	3	4	2	6*	7	8	9	10	11		5																4
		3	4	2	6	7	8	9	10	11		5	1															5
		3	4	2	6	7*	8	9			10	5	1	12	11													6
		2	4	5	6		8		10	11			1	7		9		3										7
		2	4	5	6		8	12	10	11			1	7		9*		3										8
		2	4	5	6		8		10	11			1	7		9		3										9
		5	4	2	6		8	9	10				1	7		11*	12	3										10
1		3	4	2	6	7	8	9	10	11*		5				12												11
1		2	4		6		8		10					7		9	11	3	5									12
1		2	4		6		8		10					7		9	11	3	5									13
1		2	4		6		8		10					7		9	11	3	5									14
1	3	2	4		6		8†		10	14				7	12	9	11	5*										15
	12	2	4		6*		8		10	14			1	7†	9	11		3	5									16
		5		2	6		8	12	10			4	1	7†	9	11*		3	14									17
1		2		5			8	9	10			4				11		3	6	7								18
1		2		5			8	9	10			4				11		3	6	7								19
1		2		5		4*	8	9	10			12				11		3	6	7								20
1		2		5		4	8	9	10							11		3	6	7								21
1	11	2		5		4	8	9	10*									3	6	7	12							22
1	7	2		5		4	8	9	10			12				11†	3*		6	14								23
1	11	2		5		4	8		10							9	3		6	7								24
1	14	7†		2		4	8	12	10			5				9	11	3	6*									25
1		2		5		4	8	9*	10							11	3		6	7	12							26
1		2		5		4	8*		10			14				11†	3		6		12	9						27
1		2*		5		4	8		10							11	3		6		12	9						28
1				5		4	8†		10			14				11*	3		6		12	9	2					29
1	6			2		4	8*		10	11		14		7†		9	3		5					12				30
1	6			2†		4	8		10	11*		14		7		9	3		5					12				31
1	6			2		4	8		10	11				7*		9	3		5					12				32
1	6			2		4	8		10	11*		14		7†		9	3		5					12				33
	6			2		4	8		10	11			1*	7		9	3		5					12				34
1						4	8†		10	11*		14				9	3		5	6	7			12	2			35
1						4	8		10	11*						9	3		5	6	7			12	2			36
1						4	8		10	11*		14				9	3		5	6	7			12	2†			37
1						4	8*		10	11		12				9	3		5	6	7			12	2			38
1						4	8*		10	11						9	3		5	6	7			12	2			39
1						4	8		10	11*		14				9	3		5	6	7†			12	2			40
1						4	8		10	11*						9	3		5	6	7			12	2			41
1	4*						8†		10	11		14				9	3		5	6	7			12	2			42
1	4					7*	8		10	11		14				9	3		5	6†				12	2			43
1	4					6	8		10	11*		12				9	3		5						2	7		44
1	4					7	8		10	11*						9	3		5	6				12	2			45
1	4						8†		10	11		14*				9	12		5	6					2	7		46
37	18	20	28	29	28	20	46	26	24	18	3	33	9	11	17	35	5	25	16	20	8	3	1	12	12	2		
3				1	4		4			6	1	4		6	4	1	1			2	1			2	3		9	
1		1	1		4	8	5	7		1	3		3	3			3	1		2				3		2		

27

1990-91

1	Aug	25	(h)	Brighton & HA	W	2-1	Cooper, Smith	6,865
2	Sep	1	(a)	Millwall	L	1-4	Banks	10,114
3		8	(h)	Oldham A	L	0-1		11,257
4		15	(a)	Blackburn R	W	2-1	Saville, Rammell	7,665
5		18	(a)	Notts Co	W	3-2	McCord, Saville, O'Connell	7,195
6		22	(h)	Port Vale	D	1-1	Archdeacon (pen)	8,533
7		29	(a)	Charlton A	L	1-2	Rammell	4,379
8	Oct	2	(h)	Ipswich T	W	5-1	Taggart, Archdeacon, Rammell, Agnew, Saville	6,930
9		6	(h)	Oxford U	W	3-0	Rammell, Saville, O'Connell	6,776
10		13	(a)	Portsmouth	D	0-0		8,701
11		20	(a)	West Brom A	D	1-1	Cooper	9,577
12		23	(h)	Sheffield W	D	1-1	Rammell	23,079
13		27	(h)	Swindon T	W	5-1	O'Connell, Agnew 2 (1 pen). Rammell 2	7,690
14	Nov	3	(a)	Middlesbrough	L	0-1		18,470
15		7	(a)	Bristol R	L	1-2	Banks	4,563
16		10	(h)	Leicester C	D	1-1	O'Connell	8,581
17		17	(a)	Newcastle U	D	0-0		15,548
18		24	(h)	Wolverhampton W	D	1-1	Saville	9,267
19	Dec	1	(a)	Watford	D	0-0		7,839
20		15	(a)	Brighton & HA	L	0-1		5,829
21		22	(h)	West Ham U	W	1-0	Smith	10,348
22		26	(a)	Plymouth A	D	1-1	Rammell	5,668
23		29	(a)	Hull C	W	2-1	Agnew, Deehan	7,916
24	Jan	1	(h)	Bristol C	W	2-0	Rammell, Taggart	8,961
25		12	(h)	Millwall	L	1-2	Agnew	7,857
26		19	(a)	Oldham A	L	0-2		13,849
27		23	(a)	Leicester C	L	1-2	Smith	9,027
28		26	(h)	Bristol R	W	1-0	Saville	6,197
29	Mar	2	(h)	Watford	W	2-1	Saville, Rammell	6,755
30		9	(a)	Wolverhampton W	W	5-0	Saville, Rammell, Stancliffe (og), Robinson, Agnew	15,671
31		16	(h)	Charlton A	D	1-1	O'Connell	6,373
32		19	(h)	Portsmouth	W	4-0	Saville 2, Rimmer, Agnew	4,921
33		23	(a)	Oxford U	L	0-2		4,689
34		30	(h)	Plymouth A	W	1-0	Agnew (pen)	6,142
35	Apr	1	(a)	West Ham U	L	2-3	Saville, O'Connell	24,607
36		6	(h)	Hull C	W	3-1	O'Connell 2, Rammell	6,859
37		9	(h)	Notts Co	W	1-0	O'Connell	9,801
38		13	(a)	Bristol C	L	0-1		12,081
39		15	(a)	Port Vale	W	1-0	Saville	6,939
40		20	(h)	West Brom A	D	1-1	Deehan	9,593
41		23	(h)	Blackburn R	L	0-1		8,648
42		25	(a)	Ipswich T	L	0-2		7,379
43		27	(a)	Sheffield W	L	1-3	Smith	30,693
44	May	4	(a)	Swindon T	W	2-1	Tiler, Smith	9,070
45		7	(h)	Newcastle U	D	1-1	Smith	9,543
46		11	(h)	Middlesbrough	W	1-0	Tiler	14,494

FINAL LEAGUE POSITION: 8th in Division Two

Appearances

Sub Appearances

Goals

28

Baker	Fleming	Taggart	McCord	Joyce	Smith	Banks	Cooper	Saville	Agnew	Archdeacon	Tiler	O'Connell	Robinson	Connelly	Rammell	Dobbin	Gridelet	Marshall	Deehan	Rimmer	Cross	#
1	2	3	4	5	6	7	8	9	10	11												1
1	2	3	4		5	7	8	9*	10	11	6	12										2
1	2	3	4	5*		8		9	10	11	6	12	7									3
1	2	3	4	5		8*		9†		11	6	12	7	10	14							4
1	2*	3	4	5		8†		9	10	11	6	12	7		14							5
1	2†	3	4	5		8		9		11	6	12	7	10*	14							6
1	2	3	4	5		8†		9	10	11	6	12	7*		14							7
1		3	4	5	2			9	10	11*	6	7	12		8							8
1		3	4	5	2			9	10	11	6	7			8							9
1	5	3	4		2			9	10*	11	6	7	12		8							10
1	5	3	4		2	12		9		11	6	7	10		8*							11
1	5	3	4		2			9		11	6	7	10		8							12
1	5	3*	4	12	2			9	10	11	6	7			8							13
1	5	3	4		2*	12		9	10	11	6	7			8							14
1	5*	3	4		2	12		9	10	11	6	7			8							15
1	5	3	4		2	12		9	10*	11	6	7			8							16
1	5	4	3		2			9†		11	6	7	12	10*	8	14						17
1	5	8*	3		2			9		11	6	7	10		4			12				18
1	5	8	3		2			9*		11	6	7	12	10	4							19
1	5	3	4†		2*			9	10	11	6	7	12		8	14						20
1	4	3	5		2*			9	10	11	6	7	12		8†	14						21
1	4*	3	5		2			9	10	11	6	7			8			12				22
1	4	3	5		2			9	10	11	6	7			8*			12				23
1	4	3	5		2			9	10	11	6	7			8*			12				24
1	3	4†	5*		2			9	10	11	6	7		14	8			12				25
1	3	4*	5		2			9	10	11	6	7			8			12				26
1	4	3	5		2			9	10	11	6	7			8							27
1	4	3	5		2†			9	10	11	6	7	12		8*	14						28
1	4	3†	5*		2			9	10	11	6	7			8	14		12				29
1	3	2	5	14				9	10	11	6	7†	12		8*				4			30
1	3	2*		14				9	10	11	6	7	12		8				4		5†	31
1	3	2						9	10	11	6	7*	5		8	14			4	12		32
1	3	8†	2*					9	10†	11	6	7	5		12	14			4			33
1	3		5					9	10	11	6	7			8	2			4			34
1	3		5					9	10	11	6	7	4		8†	2*			14	12		35
1	3		5					9	10	11	6	7	4*		8	2				12		36
1	3		5					9	10	11	6	7	4		8	2						37
1	4	3*	5					9	10	11	6	7	12		8	2†			14			38
1	3		5					9	10	11	6	7	2		12			8*	4			39
1	3		5					9	10†	11	6	7	2*		12	14		8*	4			40
1	3	14	5					9		11	6	7	2†	10	12			8*	4			41
1	3	12	5*		2			9	10	11	6	7			8†	14			4			42
1	3	12	2†	5	4			9*	10	11	6	7			8				14			43
1	2	3	5		4			9	10	11	6	7			8*				12			44
1	2	3*	5		4			9	10	11	6	7			8				12			45
1	2	3	5		4			9	10		6	7	11		8							46
46	44	28	23	3	36	31	8	45	38	45	45	39	15	5	32	8	1	3	10	1		
		2	1		1	2	4					6	7	4	8	6	3	1	8	5	1	
		2	1		6	2	2	12	8	2	2	9	1		12				2		1	

29

1991-92

1	Aug	17	(a)	Plymouth A	L	1-2	Pearson	6,352
2		20	(h)	Sunderland	L	0-3		12,454
3		24	(h)	Brighton & HA	L	1-2	O'Connell	6,066
4		27	(a)	Port Vale	D	0-0		6,229
5		31	(a)	Swindon T	L	1-3	Banks	7,449
6	Sep	3	(h)	Watford	L	0-3		6,500
7		7	(a)	Derby Co	D	1-1	Saville	10,559
8		14	(h)	Ipswich T	W	1-0	Currie	6,786
9		17	(h)	Leicester C	W	3-1	Rammell, Taggart, Redfearn (pen)	9,318
10		21	(a)	Tranmere R	L	1-2	Banks	8,482
11		28	(h)	Millwall	L	0-2		6,544
12	Oct	5	(a)	Wolverhampton W	W	2-1	Saville, O'Connell	14,082
13		12	(h)	Portsmouth	W	2-0	Taggart, Graham	6,579
14		19	(h)	Bristol C	L	1-2	Currie	6,566
15		26	(a)	Cambridge U	L	1-2	Rammell	5,534
16	Nov	2	(a)	Oxford U	W	1-0	Redfearn	3,419
17		5	(h)	Middlesbrough	W	2-1	Rammell, Taggart	6,525
18		9	(h)	Bristol R	L	0-1		6,688
19		16	(a)	Blackburn R	L	0-3		13,797
20		23	(a)	Southend U	L	1-2	Saville	5,060
21		30	(h)	Newcastle U	W	3-0	Saville, Robinson, Rammell	9,648
22	Dec	7	(a)	Charlton A	D	1-1	Redfearn (pen)	4,581
23		14	(h)	Grimsby T	W	4-1	Currie, Archdeacon 2, Saville	6,856
24		22	(a)	Watford	D	1-1	Robinson	8,522
25		26	(h)	Port Vale	D	0-0		8,843
26		28	(h)	Swindon T	D	1-1	Rammell	8,357
27	Jan	1	(a)	Sunderland	L	0-2		16,107
28		11	(a)	Brighton & HA	L	1-3	Currie	6,107
29		18	(h)	Plymouth A	L	1-3	Saville	5,322
30	Feb	1	(a)	Bristol C	W	2-0	Archdeacon, O'Connell	9,508
31		8	(h)	Cambridge U	D	0-0		6,196
32		15	(h)	Southend U	W	1-0	O'Connell	5,328
33		22	(a)	Newcastle U	D	1-1	Currie	27,670
34		29	(h)	Charlton A	W	1-0	Archdeacon	6,050
35	Mar	7	(a)	Grimsby T	W	1-0	Archdeacon	6,913
36		14	(h)	Oxford U	W	1-0	Currie	5,436
37		21	(a)	Bristol R	D	0-0		5,665
38		28	(h)	Blackburn R	W	2-1	Smith, Rammell	13,346
39		31	(a)	Ipswich T	L	0-2		14,148
40	Apr	4	(h)	Derby Co	L	0-3		10,121
41		11	(a)	Leicester C	L	1-3	Currie	14,438
42		13	(a)	Middlesbrough	W	1-0	Redfearn	12,743
43		18	(h)	Tranmere R	D	1-1	Archdeacon	5,811
44		22	(a)	Millwall	D	1-1	Rammell	5,703
45		26	(h)	Wolverhampton W	W	2-0	Bullimore, Rammell	7,244
46	May	2	(a)	Portsmouth	L	0-2		11,169

FINAL LEAGUE POSITION: 16th in Division Two

Appearances

Sub Appearances

Goals

Whitehead	Bishop	Williams	Banks	Davis	Taggart	O'Connell	Rammell	Pearson	McCord	Graham	Fleming	Connelly	Smith	Butler	Robinson	Cross	Redfearn	Currie	Archdeacon	Saville	Bullimore	Whitworth	Liddell	#
1	2	3	4	5	6	7	8	9	10*	11	12													1
1	2	3	4	5	6*	7	8	9		11†	10	12	14											2
1	2		4	5	6	7	8	9*		12	10	11	3											3
	10		4		6	7	8	9		11				5	1	2	3							4
	10		4		6	7	8	9*		12	11			5	1	2	3							5
	10		4	5	6	7	8			9	2	11*		1	12	3								6
	2		4*		6	7	8†	12		3				5	1			9	10	11	14			7
			4		6	7		12		3				5	1	2	8	10	11	9*				8
			4		6	7		9		3				5	1	2	8	10*	11	12				9
			4		6	7*		9		10		3		5	1	2	8		11	12				10
			4*		6	7		9				3		5	1	2	8	10	11	12				11
		12			6	7	11	9			4			1	2		8	10*	3	5				12
12					6	7	11	9	10		4			1	2		8		3*	5				13
	14				6	7	11	9*		12	4			1	2		8	10	3	5†				14
	9				6	7	11			12	4			5	1	2	8	10*	3					15
	9*				6	7	11				4			5	1	2	8	12	3			10		16
	9				6	7	11				4			5	1	2	8	10	3					17
5	9				6	7	11			12	4*				1	2	8	10	3					18
14	9*				6	7	11	12			4			5	1	2	8	10†	3					19
10					6		11				4*			5	1	2	8	12	3	9	7			20
3					6		10*					2		5	1	7	8	12	11	9	4			21
3					6					12		2		5	1	7	8	10*	11	9	4			22
3		14			6					12		2		5	1	7	8†	10*	11	9	4			23
3					6			12				2		5	1	7	8	10*	11	9	4			24
3					6			12				2		5	1	7	8	10	11	9	4*			25
	14	3			6			10				2*		5	1	7	8	12	11	9†	4			26
	3*	14			6			10				2		5	1	7	8	12	11	9	4†			27
3					6	7*		9		12		5			1	2†	8	10	11	14	4			28
3			5		6	12		7		14		2†			1		8	10	11	9	4*			29
3		8			6			7		9	4			5	1	2		10	11					30
3		8			6	7*				9	4			5	1	2		10	11	12				31
	3*	8	3*			7†				9†	4			5	1	2	14	10	11	12				32
		8	3*			7†		14			4			5	1	2	9	10	11	12		6		33
3		8						7		12	4*	14		5	1	2		10	11	9†		6		34
3		8	4					7						5	1	2		9	10	11		6		35
4	3	8						7						5	1	2		9	10	11		6		36
4	3	8						7						5	1	2		9	10	11		6		37
4	3	8						7		12				5	1	2		9	10*	11		6		38
	3	8*		4†				7		10		14		5	1	2		9	12	11		6		39
	3*	8						7		10	4	14		5	1	2		9	12	11		6†		40
		8†						7*		3	4	12		5	1	2		9	10	11	14	6		41
			3					7*			4	12		5	1	2		9	10	11	8	6		42
14			3†					7*		10	4	12		5	1	2		9	11		8	6		43
6			3					12		10*	4			5	1	2		9	7	11	8			44
6	12		3*					10			4			5	1	2		9	7	11	8			45
	6*		3					10		12	4			5	1	2		9	7†	11	8	14		46
3	25	15	23	8	38	34	31	8	1	8	40	2	37	43	40	3	35	30	40	14	17	11		
3	2	3	1		2	6	2	2		13	2	1	1		1		1	7		8	1		1	
		2			3	4	8	1		1		1	2				4	7	6	6	1			

1992-93

1	Aug	16	(h)	West Ham U	L	0-1		6,798
2		22	(a)	Portsmouth	L	0-1		11,473
3		29	(h)	Millwall	D	0-0		4,795
4	Sep	1	(h)	Wolverhampton W	L	0-1		6,906
5		5	(a)	Notts Co	W	3-1	Taggart, Liddell, Archdeacon	6,205
6		12	(h)	Derby Co	D	1-1	Rammell	8,412
7		19	(h)	Peterborough U	L	1-2	Liddell	5,275
8		26	(a)	Bristol C	L	1-2	O'Connell	8,049
9	Oct	3	(a)	Leicester C	L	1-2	Biggins	12,290
10		10	(h)	Luton T	W	3-0	Biggins 2, Pearson	5,261
11		17	(a)	Oxford U	D	0-0		4,422
12		24	(h)	Brentford	W	3-2	Biggins, Pearson 2	4,928
13		31	(a)	Swindon T	L	0-1		7,784
14	Nov	3	(a)	Bristol R	W	5-1	Robinson M, Taggart, O'Connell, Redfearn	6,100
15		7	(h)	Watford	L	0-1		6,193
16		14	(a)	Cambridge U	W	2-0	Biggins 2	3,971
17		21	(h)	Birmingham C	W	1-0	Currie	5,603
18		28	(h)	Charlton A	W	1-0	Biggins	5,851
19	Dec	5	(a)	Sunderland	L	1-2	Sampson (og)	17,395
20		13	(h)	Newcastle U	W	1-0	O'Connell	13,263
21		19	(a)	Southend U	L	0-3		3,629
22		26	(a)	Grimsby T	L	2-4	Taggart, Currie	8,242
23		28	(h)	Tranmere R	W	3-1	Currie, Rammell, Redfearn	8,204
24	Jan	9	(a)	Peterborough U	D	1-1	Rammell	6,000
25		16	(h)	Bristol C	W	2-1	O'Connell 2	5,423
26		27	(a)	Wolverhampton W	L	0-1		11,342
27		30	(h)	Portsmouth	D	1-1	Archdeacon	6,551
28	Feb	6	(a)	West Ham U	D	1-1	Rammell	14,101
29		10	(a)	Derby Co	L	0-3		13,096
30		20	(a)	Millwall	W	4-0	Archdeacon 2, Biggins 2	8,034
31		27	(a)	Luton T	D	2-2	O'Connell, Currie	7,595
32	Mar	6	(h)	Leicester C	L	2-3	Rammell 2	9,452
33		9	(h)	Cambridge U	W	2-0	Biggins, Redfearn	5,445
34		13	(a)	Watford	W	2-1	Biggins 2	5,785
35		16	(h)	Notts Co	D	0-0		6,296
36		20	(h)	Sunderland	W	2-0	Biggins 2	7,297
37		23	(a)	Birmingham C	L	0-3		12,664
38		27	(h)	Bristol R	W	2-1	Graham, Archdeacon	5,220
39	Apr	3	(a)	Charlton A	D	0-0		6,370
40		7	(a)	Newcastle U	L	0-6		29,460
41		10	(h)	Grimsby T	L	0-2		4,958
42		12	(a)	Tranmere R	L	1-2	Taggart	6,436
43		17	(h)	Southend U	W	3-1	Williams 3	3,855
44		24	(h)	Oxford U	L	0-1		5,588
45	May	1	(a)	Brentford	L	1-3	Williams	7,958
46		8	(h)	Swindon T	W	1-0	Williams	6,031

Final League Position: 13th in Division One

Appearances

Sub Appearances

Goals

Butler	Robinson M	Taggart	Bishop	Fleming	Bullimore	Currie	Rammell	Pearson	Redfearn	Archdeacon	Liddell	Smith	Graham	Burton	O'Connell	Robinson J	Biggins	Godfrey	Connelly	Williams	Watson	Davis	Whitehead	Hendon	Jackson	Gridelet	Bennett	Feeney	Eaden	
1	2	3	4	5	6	7	8*	9	10	11	12																			1
1	2	3	4	5	6†	12	8*	9	10	11	7	14																		2
1	2*	3	4	5	6†	8	12	9	10	11	7	14																		3
1	2	3	4	5	6†	8*	12	9	10	11	7	14																		4
1	14	3	4	5		12	8	9	10	11	7*	2			6†															5
1		3	4	5			8	9	10	11	7*	2			6	12														6
1		3	4	5		14	8	9†	10	11	7	2*			6	12														7
1	2	3	4	5	12	14		9	10	11	7†				6*	8														8
1		5	4†	2			8	9	10	11	14				6*	12	3	7												9
1	2		4	5	6		8*	9	10†	11						12	3	7	14											10
1	2	5	4	3	6		8*	9	10	11						12	7													11
1	2	5	4	3			8*	9	10	11					6		7		12											12
1	2	5	4	3			12	9	10	11	8*				6		7													13
1	2	5	4	3			8*		10	11	9†				6		7			14										14
1	2	5	4	3*			8		10	11	9				6		7													15
1	2	5	4	3		12		9	10	11	8*				6		7													16
1	2	5	4	3		14		9	10	11	8†				6		7													17
1	2	5	4	3		14		9	10	11	8†				6		7													18
1	2	5	4	3*		12	8	9	10	11					6		7													19
1	2	5	4	3			8	9*	10	11	12				6		7													20
1	2	5	4	3†		12	8		10	11	9*				6		7			14										21
1	2	5	4	3		7	8*		10	11	9†				6		12			14										22
1	2	5	4	3		9	8		10	11			12		6		7*													23
1	2	5	4	3		9†	8	14	10	11					6		7													24
1	2	5	4	3		9	8		10	11					6		7													25
1	2†	5	4	3		7	8	9	10	11					6					14										26
1	2	5	4	3		7	8	9	10	11					6															27
1	2	5	4	3		7†	8	9	10	11	14				6															28
	2	5	4	3		7	8		10	11					6		14	9†			1									29
	2	5		3		9	8		10	11					6		7				1	4								30
	2	5		3		9	8		10	11					6		7				1	4								31
	2†	5	4	3*		9	8		10	11	14				6		7						12	1						32
		5		3		9	8		10	11	2*		12		6		7						4	1						33
		5	2	3	14	9	8†		10	11					6		7						4	1						34
		5	2	3	8	9			10	11					6		7						4	1						35
		5	2	3		9			10	11			12		6		7						4	1	8*					36
		5	2	3	14	9*			10					11	6		7	12					4†	1	8					37
		5	4	3	14	9			10*	11			8		6†		7	14						1	2					38
		5	4	3	8	12			10				9*		6†	11	7	14						1	2					39
		5	4	3	8*	9			10				14		6†	11	7							1	2	12				40
		5	4	3	14	12			10				9		6		7						11†	1	2*		8			41
		5	4	3	8†				10				9*		6		12						11	1		14	2			42
			4	3	14				10				9			2	7					5		1	8*			6†	12	43
		5	4	3	12				10				9		6	2	7						11	1				8*		44
		5	4*	3	8				10				9†		6	2	7						11	1				14	12	45
		5	4	3	12	8			10				9		6	2†	11*						1						7	46
28	28	44	43	46	10	23	27	21	46	37	16	3	9	5	35	8	32	1		4	5	10	13	6	1	2	2		1	
1					7	12	3	1				5	1	6		5		2	5	1	4		1			2			2	1	
	1	4				4	6	3	3	5	2		1			6		14			5									

33

F.A. CUP COMPETITION

1983/84 SEASON
3rd Round
Jan 7 vs Sheffield Wednesday (a) 0-1
Att: 29,638

1984/85 SEASON
3rd Round
Jan 5 vs Reading (h) 4-3
Att: 7,272   Futcher R., Owen 2 (1 pen), Joyce

4th Round
Jan 26 vs Brighton & Hove Albion (h) 2-1
Att: 8,860   Owen, Futcher R.

5th Round
Mar 4 vs Southampton (a) 2-1
Att: 20,971   Agnew, Owen (pen)

6th Round
Mar 10 vs Liverpool (h) 0-4
Att: 19,838

1985/86 SEASON
3rd Round
Jan 13 vs Bury (a) 0-2
Att: 3,676

1986/87 SEASON
3rd Round
Jan 10 vs Caernarfon (a) 0-0
Att: 2,630

Replay
Jan 26 vs Caernarfon (h) 1-0
Att: 8,530   Wylde

4th Round
Jan 31 vs Aldershot (a) 1-1
Att: 4,772   Agnew

Replay
Feb 3 vs Aldershot (h) 3-0
Att: 9,784   May 2, Thomas

5th Round
Feb 21 vs Arsenal (a) 0-2
Att: 28,302

1987/88 SEASON
3rd Round
Jan 9 vs Bolton Wanderers (h) 3-1
Att: 9,667   Broddle 2, Beresford

4th Round
Jan 30 vs Birmingham City (h) 0-2
Att: 13,219

1988/89 SEASON
3rd Round
Jan 7 vs Chelsea (h) 4-0
Att: 13,241   Thomas, Agnew 2, Currie

4th Round
Jan 28 vs Stoke City (a) 3-3
Att: 18,592   Currie 2, MacDonald

Replay
Jan 31 vs Stoke City (h) 2-1
Att: 21,086   MacDonald, Cooper

5th Round
Feb 18 vs Everton (h) 0-1
Att: 32,551

1989/90 SEASON
3rd Round
Jan 6 vs Leicester City (a) 2-1
Att: 16,278   Currie, Lowndes

4th Round
Jan 27 vs Ipswich Town (h) 2-0
Att: 14,440   Taggart, Cooper

5th Round
Feb 18 vs Sheffield United (a) 2-2
Att: 33,113   Smith, Cooper

Replay
Feb 21 vs Sheffield United (h) 0-0 (aet.)
Att: 27,672

2nd Replay
Mar 5 vs Sheffield United (h) 0-1 (aet.)
Att: 26,560

1990/91 SEASON
3rd Round
Jan 6 vs Leeds United (h) 1-1
Att: 22,424   Deehan

Replay
Jan 9 vs Leeds United (a) 0-4
Att: 19,773

1991/92 SEASON
3rd Round
Jan 4 vs Norwich City (a) 0-1
Att: 12,189

1992/93 SEASON
3rd Round
Jan 13 vs Leicester City (a) 2-2
Att: 19,137   Whitlow (og), Redfearn

Replay
Jan 20 vs Leicester City (h) 1-1 (aet.)
Barnsley win 5-4 on penalties
Att: 15,423   Archdeacon

4th Round
Jan 24 vs West Ham United (h) 4-1
Att: 13,716   Rammell 3, Redfearn

5th Round
Feb 13 vs Manchester City (a) 0-2
Att: 32,807

LEAGUE CUP COMPETITION

1983/84 SEASON
2nd Round (1st leg)
Oct 3 vs Walsall (a) 0-1
Att: 3,681

2nd Round (2nd leg)
Oct 25 vs Walsall (h) 0-2 (aggregate 0-3)
Att: 7,844

1984/85 SEASON
2nd Round (1st leg)
Sep 25 vs Grimsby Town (a) 0-3
Att: 3,577

2nd Round (2nd leg)
Oct 9 vs Grimsby Town (h) 1-1 (aggregate 1-4)
Att: 5,578   Foley

1985/86 SEASON
2nd Round (1st leg)
Sep 25 vs Newcastle United (a) 0-0
Att: 18,544

2nd Round (2nd leg)
Oct 7 vs Newcastle United (h) 1-1 (aggregate 1-1)
Att: 10,084   Gray (pen)
Newcastle win on away goals

1986/87 SEASON
2nd Round (1st leg)
Sep 23 vs Tottenham Hotspur (h) 2-3
Att: 9,979   Gray 2 (1 pen)

2nd Round (2nd leg)
Oct 8 vs Tottenham Hotspur (a) 3-5 (agg. 8-5)
Att: 12,299   Beresford, May, Chandler

1987/88 SEASON
2nd Round (1st leg)
Sep 22 vs West Ham United (h) 0-0
Att: 10,330

2nd Round (2nd leg)
Oct 6 vs West Ham United (a) 5-2 (aet.) (agg. 5-2)
Att: 12,403   Agnew 2 (1 pen), Beresford,
Lowndes, MacDonald

3rd Round
Oct 27 vs Sheffield Wednesday (h) 1-2
Att: 19,439   Agnew

1988/89 SEASON
2nd Round (1st leg)
Sep 27 vs Wimbledon (h) 0-2
Att: 5,194

2nd Round (2nd leg)
Oct 12 vs Wimbledon (a) 1-0 (aggregate 1-2)
Att: 2,259   Currie

1989/90 SEASON
2nd Round (1st leg)
Sep 19 vs Blackpool (h) 1-1
Att: 7,515   Archdeacon

2nd Round (2nd leg)
Oct 3 vs Blackpool (a) 1-1 (aet.) (aggregate 2-2)
Att: 5,251   Briggs (og)
Blackpool won 5-4 on penalties

1990/91 SEASON
1st Round (1st leg)
Aug 28 vs Wigan Athletic (a) 1-0
Att: 2,144   Cooper

1st Round (2nd leg)
Sep 4 vs Wigan Athletic (h) 0-1 (aet.) (agg. 1-1)
Att: 4,558   Barnsley won 4-3 on penalties

2nd Round (1st leg)
Sep 26 vs Aston Villa (a) 0-1
Att: 14,471

2nd Round (2nd leg)
Oct 9 vs Aston Villa (h) 0-1 (aggregate 0-2)
Att: 13,924

1991/92 SEASON
2nd Round (1st leg)
Sep 24 vs Blackpool (a) 0-1
Att: 4,123

2nd Round (2nd leg)
Oct 8 vs Blackpool (h) 2-0 (aggregate 2-1)
Att: 6,315   O'Connell, Pearson

3rd Round
Oct 29 vs Middlesbrough (a) 0-1
Att: 9,381

1992/93 SEASON
1st Round (1st leg)
Aug 19 vs Grimsby Town (a) 1-1
Att: 3,927   Redfearn

1st Round (2nd leg)
Aug 25 vs Grimsby Town (h) 1-1 (aet.) (agg. 2-2)
Att: 4,636   Liddell. Grimsby win 5-3 on penalties

1983-84 SEASON
SECOND DIVISION

	P	W	D	L	F	A	Pts
Chelsea	42	25	13	4	90	40	89
Sheffield Wednesday	42	26	10	6	72	34	89
Newcastle United	42	24	8	10	85	53	80
Manchester City	42	20	10	12	66	48	70
Grimsby Town	42	19	13	10	60	47	70
Blackburn Rovers	42	17	16	9	57	46	67
Carlisle United	42	16	16	10	48	41	64
Shrewsbury Town	42	17	10	15	49	53	61
Brighton & Hove Alb.	42	17	9	16	69	60	60
Leeds United	42	16	12	14	55	56	60
Fulham	42	15	12	15	60	53	57
Huddersfield Town	42	14	15	13	56	49	57
Charlton Athletic	42	16	9	17	53	64	57
Barnsley	**42**	**15**	**7**	**20**	**57**	**53**	**52**
Cardiff City	42	15	6	21	53	66	51
Portsmouth	42	14	7	21	73	64	49
Middlesbrough	42	12	13	17	41	47	49
Crystal Palace	42	12	11	19	42	52	47
Oldham Athletic	42	13	8	21	47	73	47
Derby County	42	11	9	22	36	72	42
Swansea City	42	7	8	27	36	85	29
Cambridge United	42	4	12	26	28	77	24

1984-85 SEASON
SECOND DIVISION

	P	W	D	L	F	A	Pts
Oxford United	42	25	9	8	84	36	84
Birmingham City	42	25	7	10	59	33	82
Manchester City	42	21	11	10	66	40	74
Portsmouth	42	20	14	8	69	50	74
Blackburn Rovers	42	21	10	11	66	41	73
Brighton & Hove Alb.	42	20	12	10	58	34	72
Leeds United	42	19	12	11	66	43	69
Shrewsbury Town	42	18	11	13	66	53	65
Fulham	42	19	8	15	68	64	65
Grimsby Town	42	18	8	16	72	64	62
Barnsley	**42**	**14**	**16**	**12**	**42**	**42**	**58**
Wimbledon	42	16	10	16	71	75	58
Huddersfield Town	42	15	10	17	52	64	55
Oldham Athletic	42	15	8	19	49	67	53
Crystal Palace	42	12	12	18	46	65	48
Carlisle United	42	13	8	21	50	67	47
Charlton Athletic	42	11	12	19	51	63	45
Sheffield United	42	10	14	18	54	66	44
Middlesbrough	42	10	10	22	41	57	40
Notts County	42	10	7	25	45	73	37
Cardiff	42	9	8	25	47	79	35
Wolves	42	8	9	25	37	79	33

1985-86 SEASON
SECOND DIVISION

	P	W	D	L	F	A	Pts
Norwich City	42	25	9	8	84	39	84
Charlton Athletic	42	22	11	9	78	45	77
Wimbledon	42	21	13	8	58	37	76
Portsmouth	42	22	7	13	69	41	73
Crystal Palace	42	19	9	14	57	52	66
Hull City	42	17	13	12	65	55	64
Sheffield United	42	17	11	14	64	63	62
Oldham Athletic	42	17	9	16	62	61	60
Millwall	42	17	8	17	64	65	59
Stoke City	42	14	15	13	48	50	57
Brighton & Hove Alb.	42	16	8	18	64	64	56
Barnsley	**42**	**14**	**14**	**14**	**47**	**50**	**56**
Bradford City	42	16	6	20	51	63	54
Leeds United	42	15	8	19	56	72	53
Grimsby Town	42	14	10	18	58	62	52
Huddersfield Town	42	14	10	18	51	67	52
Shrewsbury Town	42	14	9	19	52	64	51
Sunderland	42	13	11	18	47	61	50
Blackburn Rovers	42	12	13	17	53	62	49
Carlisle United	42	13	7	22	47	71	46
Middlesbrough	42	12	9	21	44	53	45
Fulham	42	10	6	26	45	69	36

1986-87 SEASON
SECOND DIVISION

	P	W	D	L	F	A	Pts
Derby County	42	25	9	8	64	38	84
Portsmouth	42	23	9	10	53	28	78
Oldham Athletic	42	22	9	11	65	44	75
Leeds United	42	19	11	12	58	44	68
Ipswich Town	42	17	13	12	59	43	64
Crystal Palace	42	19	5	18	51	53	62
Plymouth Argyle	42	16	13	13	62	57	61
Stoke City	42	16	10	16	63	53	58
Sheffield United	42	15	13	14	50	49	58
Bradford City	42	15	10	17	62	62	55
Barnsley	**42**	**14**	**13**	**15**	**49**	**52**	**55**
Blackburn Rovers	42	15	10	17	45	55	55
Reading	42	14	11	17	52	59	53
Hull City	42	13	14	15	41	55	53
West Brom	42	13	12	17	51	49	51
Millwall	42	14	9	19	39	45	51
Huddersfield Town	42	13	12	17	54	61	51
Shrewsbury Town	42	15	6	21	41	63	51
Birmingham City	42	11	17	14	47	59	50
Sunderland	42	12	12	18	49	59	48
Grimsby Town	42	10	14	18	39	59	44
Brighton & Hove Alb.	42	9	12	21	37	54	39

1987-88 SEASON
SECOND DIVISION

Millwall	44	25	7	12	72	52	82
Aston Villa	44	22	12	10	68	41	78
Middlesbrough	44	22	12	10	63	36	78
Bradford City	44	22	11	11	74	54	77
Blackburn Rovers	44	21	14	9	68	52	77
Crystal Palace	44	22	9	13	86	59	75
Leeds United	44	19	12	13	61	51	69
Ipswich Town	44	19	9	16	61	52	66
Manchester City	44	19	8	17	80	60	65
Oldham Athletic	44	18	11	15	72	64	65
Stoke City	44	17	11	16	50	57	62
Swindon Town	44	16	11	17	73	60	59
Leicester City	44	16	11	17	62	61	59
Barnsley	**44**	**15**	**12**	**17**	**61**	**62**	**57**
Hull City	44	14	15	15	54	60	57
Plymouth Argyle	44	16	8	20	65	67	56
Bournemouth	44	13	10	21	56	68	49
Shrewsbury Town	44	11	16	17	42	54	49
Birmingham City	44	11	15	18	41	66	48
West Brom	44	12	11	21	50	69	47
Sheffield United	44	13	7	24	45	74	46
Reading	44	10	12	22	44	70	42
Huddersfield Town	44	6	10	28	41	100	28

1988-89 SEASON
SECOND DIVISION

Chelsea	46	29	12	5	96	50	99
Manchester City	46	23	13	10	77	53	82
Crystal Palace	46	23	12	11	71	49	81
Watford	46	22	12	12	74	48	78
Blackburn Rovers	46	22	11	13	74	59	77
Swindon Town	46	20	16	10	68	53	76
Barnsley	**46**	**20**	**14**	**12**	**66**	**58**	**74**
Ipswich Town	46	22	7	17	71	61	73
West Brom	46	18	18	10	65	41	72
Leeds United	46	17	16	13	59	50	67
Sunderland	46	16	15	15	60	60	63
Bournemouth	46	18	8	20	53	62	62
Stoke City	46	15	14	17	57	72	59
Bradford City	46	13	17	16	52	59	56
Leicester City	46	13	16	17	56	63	55
Oldham Athletic	46	11	21	14	75	72	54
Oxford United	46	14	12	20	62	70	54
Plymouth Argyle	46	14	12	20	55	66	54
Brighton & Hove Alb.	46	14	9	23	57	66	51
Portsmouth	46	13	12	21	53	62	51
Hull City	46	11	14	21	52	68	47
Shrewsbury Town	46	8	18	20	40	67	42
Birmingham City	46	8	11	27	31	76	35
Walsall	46	5	16	25	41	80	31

1988-90 SEASON
SECOND DIVISION

Leeds United	46	24	13	9	79	52	85
Sheffield United	46	24	13	9	78	58	85
Newcastle United	46	22	14	10	80	55	80
Swindon Town	46	20	14	12	79	59	74
Blackburn Rovers	46	19	17	10	74	59	74
Sunderland	46	20	14	12	70	64	74
West Ham United	46	20	12	14	80	57	72
Oldham Athletic	46	19	14	13	70	57	71
Ipswich Town	46	19	12	15	67	66	69
Wolves	46	18	13	15	67	60	67
Port Vale	46	15	16	15	62	57	61
Portsmouth	46	15	16	15	62	65	61
Leicester City	46	15	14	17	67	79	59
Hull City	46	14	16	16	58	65	58
Watford	46	14	15	17	58	60	57
Plymouth Argyle	46	14	13	19	58	63	55
Oxford United	46	15	9	22	57	66	54
Brighton & Hove Alb.	46	15	9	22	56	72	54
Barnsley	**46**	**13**	**15**	**18**	**49**	**71**	**54**
West Brom	46	12	15	19	67	71	51
Middlesbrough	46	13	11	22	52	63	50
Bournemouth	46	12	12	22	57	76	48
Bradford City	46	9	14	23	44	68	41
Stoke City	46	6	19	21	35	63	37

1990-91 SEASON
SECOND DIVISION

Oldham Athletic	46	25	13	8	83	53	88
West Ham United	46	24	15	7	60	34	87
Sheffield Wednesday	46	22	16	8	80	51	82
Notts County	46	23	11	12	76	55	80
Millwall	46	20	13	13	70	51	73
Brighton & Hove Alb.	46	21	7	18	63	69	70
Middlesbrough	46	20	9	17	66	47	69
Barnsley	**46**	**19**	**12**	**15**	**63**	**48**	**69**
Bristol City	46	20	7	19	68	71	67
Oxford United	46	14	19	13	69	66	61
Newcastle United	46	14	17	15	49	56	59
Wolves	46	13	19	14	63	63	58
Bristol Rovers	46	15	13	18	56	59	58
Ipswich Town	46	13	18	15	60	68	57
Port Vale	46	15	12	19	56	64	57
Charlton Athletic	46	13	17	16	57	61	56
Portsmouth	46	14	11	21	58	70	53
Plymouth Argyle	46	12	17	17	54	68	53
Blackburn Rovers	46	14	10	22	51	66	52
Watford	46	12	15	19	45	59	51
Swindon Town	46	12	14	20	65	73	50
Leicester City	46	14	8	24	60	83	50
West Brom	46	10	18	18	52	61	48
Hull City	46	10	15	21	57	85	45

37

1991-92 SEASON

SECOND DIVISION

Ipswich Town	46	24	12	10	70	50	84
Middlesbrough	46	23	11	12	58	41	80
Derby County	46	23	9	14	69	51	78
Leicester City	46	23	8	15	62	55	77
Cambridge United	46	19	17	10	65	47	74
Blackburn Rvrs	46	21	11	14	70	53	74
Charlton Athletic	46	20	11	15	54	48	71
Swindon Town	46	18	15	13	69	55	69
Portsmouth	46	19	12	15	65	51	69
Watford	46	18	11	17	51	48	65
Wolves	46	18	10	18	61	54	64
Southend United	46	17	11	18	63	63	62
Bristol Rovers	46	16	14	16	60	63	62
Tranmere Rovers	46	14	19	13	56	56	61
Millwall	46	17	10	19	64	71	61
Barnsley	**46**	**16**	**11**	**19**	**46**	**57**	**59**
Bristol City	46	13	15	18	55	71	54
Sunderland	46	14	11	21	61	65	53
Grimsby Town	46	14	11	21	47	62	53
Newcastle United	46	13	13	20	66	84	52
Oxford United	46	13	11	22	66	73	50
Plymouth Argyle	46	13	9	24	42	64	48
Brighton & Hove Alb.	46	12	11	23	56	77	47
Port Vale	46	10	15	21	42	59	45

1992-93 SEASON

FIRST DIVISION

Newcastle United	46	29	9	8	92	38	96
West Ham United	46	26	10	10	81	41	88
Portsmouth	46	26	10	10	80	46	88
Tranmere Rovers	46	23	10	13	72	56	79
Swindon Town	46	21	13	12	74	59	76
Leicester City	46	22	10	14	71	64	76
Millwall	46	18	16	12	65	53	70
Derby County	46	19	9	18	68	57	66
Grimsby Town	46	19	7	20	58	57	64
Peterborough United	46	16	14	16	55	63	62
Wolves	46	16	13	17	57	56	61
Charlton Athletic	46	16	13	17	49	46	61
Barnsley	**46**	**17**	**9**	**20**	**56**	**60**	**60**
Oxford United	46	14	14	18	53	56	56
Bristol City	46	14	14	18	49	67	56
Watford	46	14	13	19	57	71	55
Notts County	46	12	16	18	55	70	52
Southend United	46	13	13	20	54	64	52
Birmingham City	46	13	12	21	50	72	51
Luton Town	46	10	21	15	48	62	51
Sunderland	46	13	11	22	50	64	50
Brentford	46	13	10	23	52	71	49
Cambridge United	46	11	16	19	48	69	49
Bristol Rovers	46	10	11	25	55	87	41

Gerry Taggart
holder of the club record of
international appearances
(for Northern Ireland)

AGNEW, Stephen M.
Shipley, 9th November 1965

Source	Season	Club	Apps.	Gls
App	1983-84	Barnsley	1	-
	1984-85		10	1
	1985-86		2	-
	1986-87		33	-
	1987-88		25	6
	1988-89		39	6
	1989-90		46	8
	1990-91		38	8
Tr	1991-92	Blackburn R	2	-
	1992-93		-	-
L	1992-93	Portsmouth	5	-
Tr	1992-93	Leicester C	9	1

AIREY, Carl
Wakefield, 6th February 1965

Source	Season	Club	Apps.	Gls
App	1982-83	Barnsley	11	2
	1983-84		27	3
L	1984-85	Bradford C	5	-
Tr	1985-86	Darlington	41	16
	1986-87		34	12
From Charleroi (Belgium)				
	1986-87	Chesterfield	26	4
Tr	1987-88	Rotherham U	32	11
From Charleroi				
Tr	1988-89	Torquay U	17	3
	1989-90		12	8
L	1989-90	Shamrock R	-	-

ARCHDEACON, Owen D.
Greenock, 4th March 1966

Source	Season	Club	Apps.	Gls
	1983-89	Glasgow Celtic	76	7
Tr	1989-90	Barnsley	21	3
	1990-91		45	2
	1991-92		40	6
	1992-93		38	6

AYLOTT, Trevor K. C.
Bermondsey, 27th November 1957

Source	Season	Club	Apps.	Gls
App	1976-77	Chelsea	-	-
L	1976-77	QPR	-	-
	1977-78	Chelsea	11	2
	1978-79		15	-
	1979-80		3	-
Tr	1979-80	Barnsley	18	4
	1980-81		37	11
	1981-82		41	11
Tr	1982-83	Millwall	32	5
Tr	1982-83	Luton T	12	2
	1983-84		20	8
Tr	1984-85	Crystal Palace	35	8
	1985-86		18	4
L	1985-86	Barnsley	9	-
Tr	1986-87	Bournemouth	37	10
	1987-88		43	9
	1988-89		40	6
	1989-90		18	2
	1990-91		9	-
Tr	1990-91	Birmingham C	25	-
	1991-92		2	-
Tr	1991-92	Oxford U	37	6
Tr	1992-93	Gillingham	10	2

BAKER, Clive E.
North Walsham, 14th March 1959

Source	Season	Club	Apps.	Gls
Jnrs	1977-78	Norwich C	2	-
	1978-79		2	-
	1980-81		10	-
Tr	1984-85	Barnsley	37	-
	1985-86		42	-
	1986-87		39	-
	1987-88		44	-
	1988-89		46	-
	1989-90		37	-
	1990-91		46	-
Tr	1991-92	Coventry	-	-
Tr	1992-93	Ipswich T	31	-

Clive Baker
(pictured 1984-85 season) popular goalkeeper
photo courtesy of Barnsley Chronicle

BANKS, Ian F.
Mexborough, 9th January 1961

Source	Season	Club	Apps	Gls
App	1978-79	Barnsley	2	-
	1979-80		38	3
	1980-81		45	14
	1981-82		42	15
	1982-83		37	5
Tr	1983-84	Leicester C	26	3
	1984-85		33	9
	1985-86		31	2
	1986-87		3	-
Tr	1986-87	Huddersfield T	37	8
	1987-88		41	9
Tr	1988-89	Bradford C	30	3
Tr	1988-89	West Brom A	4	-
Tr	1989-90	Barnsley	37	3
	1990-91		33	2
	1991-92		26	2
Tr	1992-93	Rotherham U	45	5

BENNETT, Troy
Barnsley, 25th December 1975

Source	Season	Club	Apps	Gls
YT	1992-93	Barnsley	2	-

BERESFORD, John
Sheffield, 4th September 1966

Source	Season	Club	Apps	Gls
App	1983-86	Manchester C	-	-
Tr	1986-87	Barnsley	27	1
	1987-88		34	3
	1988-89		27	1
Tr	1988-89	Portsmouth	2	-
	1989-90		28	-
	1990-91		42	2
	1991-92		35	6
Tr	1992-93	Newcastle U	42	1

BIGGINS, Wayne
Sheffield, 20th November 1961

Source	Season	Club	Apps	Gls
App	1979-80	Lincoln C	-	-
	1980-81		8	1
From Matlock Town and King's Lynn				
	1983-84	Burnley	20	8
	1984-85		46	18
	1985-86		12	3
Tr	1985-86	Norwich C	28	7
	1986-87		31	4
	1987-88		20	5
Tr	1988-89	Manchester C	32	9
Tr	1989-90	Stoke C	35	10
	1990-91		38	12
	1991-92		41	22
	1992-93		8	2
Tr	1992-93	Barnsley	34	14

BISHOP, Charles D.
Nottingham, 16th February 1968

From Apprentice, Stoke City

Source	Season	Club	Apps	Gls
	1986-87	Watford	-	-
Tr	1987-88	Bury	17	-
	1988-89		38	3
	1989-90		30	1
	1990-91		29	2
Tr	1991-92	Barnsley	28	-
	1992-93		43	-

BLAIR, Andrew
Kirkcaldy, 18th December 1959

Source	Season	Club	Apps	Gls
App	1978-79	Coventry C	26	1
	1979-80		32	1
	1980-81		35	4
Tr	1981-82	Aston Villa	18	-
	1982-83		7	-
	1983-84		9	-
L	1983-84	Wolverhampton W	10	-
Tr	1984-85	Sheffield W	41	3
	1985-86		17	-
Tr	1985-86	Aston Villa	12	-
	1986-87		4	-
	1987-88		4	1
L	1987-88	Barnsley	6	-
Tr	1988-89	Northampton T	3	-

BRADSHAW, Carl
Sheffield, 2nd October 1968

Source	Season	Club	Apps	Gls
App	1986-87	Sheffield W	9	2
L	1986-87	Barnsley	6	1
	1987-88	Sheffield W	20	2
	1988-89		3	-
Tr	1988-89	Manchester C	5	-
Tr	1989-90	Sheffield U	30	3
	1990-91		27	1
	1991-92		18	2
	1992-93		32	1

BRODDLE, Julian R.
Laughton, 1st November 1964

Source	Season	Club	Apps	Gls
App	1981-82	Sheffield U	1	-
Tr	1983-84	Scunthorpe U	13	1
	1984-85		45	14
	1985-86		41	7
	1986-87		38	10
	1987-88		7	-
Tr	1987-88	Barnsley	19	1
	1988-89		38	3
	1989-90		20	-
Tr	1989-90	Plymouth A	9	-
L	1990-91	Bradford C	-	-
Tr	1990-91	St. Mirren	10	-
	1991-92		35	2
Tr	1992-93	Partick T	6	-
L	1992-93	Scunthorpe U	5	-

Source	Season	Club	Apps.	Gls

BULLIMORE, Wayne A.
Sutton-in-Ashfield, 12th September 1970

Source	Season	Club	Apps.	Gls
YT	1988-91	Manchester U	-	-
Tr	1990-91	Barnsley	-	-
	1991-92		18	1
	1992-93		17	-

BURNS, Kenneth
Glasgow, 23rd September 1953

Source	Season	Club	Apps.	Gls
App	1971-72	Birmingham C	8	-
	1972-73		14	3
	1973-74		37	10
	1974-75		39	8
	1975-76		36	5
	1976-77		36	19
Tr	1977-78	Nottingham F	41	4
	1978-79		25	-
	1979-80		34	3
	1980-81		30	5
	1981-82		7	1
Tr	1981-82	Leeds U	23	-
	1982-83		20	2
L	1982-83	Derby Co	7	1
	1983-84	Leeds U	13	-
Tr	1983-84	Derby Co	11	-
	1984-85		20	1
L	1984-85	Notts Co	2	-
Tr	1985-86	Barnsley	22	-

BURTON, Mark
Barnsley, 7th May 1973

Source	Season	Club	Apps.	Gls
YT	1991-92	Barnsley	-	-
	1992-93		5	-

BUTLER, Lee S.
Sheffield, 30th June 1966

From Harworth C.I.

Source	Season	Club	Apps.	Gls
	1986-87	Lincoln C	30	-
Tr	1987-88	Aston Villa	-	-
	1988-89		4	-
	1990-91		4	-
L	1990-91	Hull C	4	-
Tr	1991-92	Barnsley	43	-
	1992-93		28	-

CAMPBELL, Winston R.
Sheffield, 9th October 1962

Source	Season	Club	Apps.	Gls
App	1979-80	Barnsley	1	-
	1980-81		1	-
	1981-82		7	-
	1982-83		17	3
L	1982-83	Doncaster R	3	-
	1983-84	Barnsley	31	2
	1984-85		38	3
	1985-86		29	1

CHAMBERS, Philip M.
Barnsley, 10th November 1953

Source	Season	Club	Apps.	Gls
App	1970-71	Barnsley	3	-
	1971-72		7	-
	1972-73		46	1
	1973-74		46	1
	1974-75		46	2
	1975-76		30	1
	1976-77		9	1
	1977-78		10	-
	1978-79		45	1
	1979-80		32	-
	1980-81		43	-
	1981-82		42	-
	1982-83		40	-
	1983-84		37	1
	1984-85		7	-
Tr	1985-86	Rochdale	10	-
Tr	1985-86	Hartlepool U	29	-

CHANDLER, Ian
Sunderland, 20th March 1968

Source	Season	Club	Apps.	Gls
Jnrs	1986-87	Barnsley	12	-
L	1987-88	Stockport Co	5	-
Tr	1988-89	Aldershot	9	2

CLARKE, Michael D.
Birmingham, 22nd December 1967

Source	Season	Club	Apps.	Gls
App	1986-87	Barnsley	23	3
	1987-88		14	-
	1988-89		3	-
Tr	1989-90	Scarborough	36	1
	1990-91		1	-

COATSWORTH, Gary
Sunderland, 7th October 1968

Source	Season	Club	Apps.	Gls
Jnrs	1987-88	Barnsley	6	-
Tr	1989-90	Darlington	3	1
	1990-91		12	1
	1991-92		10	1
Tr	1991-92	Leicester C	3	-
	1992-93		10	2

CONNELLY, Dean
Glasgow, 6th January 1970

Source	Season	Club	Apps.	Gls
YT	1987-90	Arsenal	-	-
Tr	1990-91	Barnsley	9	-
	1991-92		3	-
Tr	1991-92	Wigan A	12	2
	1992-93	Barnsley	1	-
L	1992-93	Carlisle U	3	-
Tr	1992-93	Wigan A	7	-

COOPER, Stephen B.

Birmingham, 22nd June 1964

From Birmingham City

Source	Season	Club	Apps.	Gls
L	1983-84	Halifax T	7	1
L	1984-85	Mansfield T	-	-
Tr	1984-85	Newport Co	38	11
Tr	1985-86	Plymouth A	38	8
	1986-87		12	4
	1987-88		23	3
Tr	1988-89	Barnsley	35	6
	1989-90		30	5
	1990-91		12	2
Tr	1990-91	Tranmere R	17	2
	1991-92		9	1
L	1991-92	Peterborough U	9	-
	1992-93	Tranmere R	6	-
L	1992-93	Wigan A	4	-

CROSS, Paul

Barnsley, 31st October 1965

Source	Season	Club	Apps.	Gls
App	1984-85	Barnsley	1	-
	1985-86		20	-
	1986-87		18	-
	1987-88		38	-
	1989-90		36	-
	1990-91		2	-
	1991-92		3	-
L	1991-92	Preston N.E.	5	-
Tr	1991-92	Hartlepool U	21	-
	1992-93		37	1

CUNNINGHAM, Anthony E.

Jamaica, 12th November 1959

From Stourbridge

Source	Season	Club	Apps.	Gls
	1979-80	Lincoln C	38	12
	1980-81		34	6
	1981-82		46	11
	1982-83		5	3
Tr	1982-83	Barnsley	29	7
	1983-84		13	4
Tr	1983-84	Sheffield W	28	5
Tr	1984-85	Manchester C	18	1
Tr	1984-85	Newcastle U	13	1
	1985-86		17	1
	1986-87		17	2
Tr	1987-88	Blackpool	40	10
	1988-89		31	7
Tr	1989-90	Bury	25	8
	1990-91		33	9
Tr	1990-91	Bolton W	9	4
Tr	1991-92	Rotherham U	36	18
	1992-93		33	6

CURRIE, David N.

Stockton, 27th November 1962

Source	Season	Club	Apps.	Gls
Local	1981-82	Middlesbrough	1	-
	1982-83		8	-

Source	Season	Club	Apps.	Gls
	1983-84		39	15
	1984-85		39	12
	1985-86		26	4
Tr	1986-87	Darlington	45	12
	1987-88		31	21
Tr	1987-88	Barnsley	15	7
	1988-89		41	16
	1989-90		24	7
Tr	1989-90	Nottingham F	8	1
Tr	1990-91	Oldham A	27	2
	1991-92		4	1
Tr	1991-92	Barnsley	37	7
	1992-93		35	4
L	1992-93	Rotherham U	5	2

DAVIS, Stephen P.

Birmingham, 26th July 1965

From Apprentice, Stoke City

Source	Season	Club	Apps.	Gls
	1983-84	Crewe Alex	24	-
	1984-85		40	-
	1985-86		45	1
	1986-87		33	-
	1987-88		3	-
Tr	1987-88	Burnley	33	5
	1988-89		37	-
	1989-90		31	1
	1990-91		46	5
Tr	1991-92	Barnsley	9	-
	1992-93		11	-

DEEHAN, John M.

Birmingham, 6th August 1957

Source	Season	Club	Apps.	Gls
App	1975-76	Aston Villa	15	7
	1976-77		27	13
	1977-78		36	12
	1978-79		26	10
	1979-80		6	-
Tr	1979-80	West Brom A	28	3
	1980-81		15	2
	1981-82		4	-
Tr	1981-82	Norwich C	22	10
	1982-83		40	20
	1983-84		34	15
	1984-85		40	13
	1985-86		26	4
Tr	1986-87	Ipswich T	29	10
	1987-88		20	1
Tr	1988-89	Manchester C	-	-
Tr	1989-90	Barnsley	-	-
	1990-91		11	2

DOBBIN, James

Dunfermline, 17th September 1963

Source	Season	Club	Apps.	Gls
Celtic	1983-84	Doncaster R	11	2
	1984-85		17	1
	1985-86		31	6
	1986-87		5	4
Tr	1986-87	Barnsley	30	4
	1987-88		16	2

Source	Season	Club	Apps.	Gls
	1988-89	Barnsley	41	5
	1989-90		28	1
	1990-91		14	-
Tr	1991-92	Grimsby T	32	6
	1992-93		39	6

DUGGAN, Andrew J.

Bradford, 19th September 1967

Source	Season	Club	Apps.	Gls
YT	1986-87	Barnsley	2	1
L	1987-88	Rochdale	3	-
Tr	1988-89	Huddersfield T	14	2
	1989-90		15	1
L	1990-91	Hartlepool U	2	-
Tr	1990-91	Rochdale	1	-

DUNPHY, Sean

Maltby, 5th November 1970

Source	Season	Club	Apps.	Gls
YT	1989-90	Barnsley	6	-
Tr	1990-91	Lincoln C	-	-
	1991-92		5	1
	1992-93		31	1

EADEN, Nicky

Sheffield, 12th December 1972

Source	Season	Club	Apps.	Gls
YT	1991-92	Barnsley	-	-
	1992-93		2	-

FEENEY, Mark

Derry, 26th July 1974

Source	Season	Club	Apps.	Gls
YT	1992-93	Barnsley	2	-

FERRY, William (Willie)

Sunderland, 21st November 1966

Source	Season	Club	Apps.	Gls
YT	1984-85	Scunthorpe	1	-
	1985-86		2	-
	1986-87		2	-
Tr	1986-87	Barnsley	4	1

FINDLAY, John W.

Blairgowrie, 13th July 1954

Source	Season	Club	Apps.	Gls
App	1973-74	Aston Villa	1	-
	1974-75		1	-
	1975-76		5	-
	1976-77		7	-
Tr	1978-79	Luton T	23	-
	1979-80		41	-
	1980-81		40	-
	1981-82		34	-
	1982-83		26	-
L	1983-84	Barnsley	6	-
L	1983-84	Derby Co	1	-
	1984-85	Luton T	3	-
Tr	1985-86	Swindon T	4	-
Tr	1985-86	Portsmouth	-	-

Source	Season	Club	Apps.	Gls
Tr	1985-86	Peterborough U	-	-
Tr	1986-87	Coventry C	-	-

FLEMING, Gary J.

Londonderry, 17th February 1967

Source	Season	Club	Apps.	Gls
App	1984-85	Nottingham F	2	-
	1985-86		16	-
	1986-87		34	-
	1987-88		22	-
Tr	1989-90	Manchester C	14	-
L	1989-90	Notts Co	3	-
Tr	1989-90	Barnsley	12	-
	1990-91		44	-
	1991-92		42	-
	1992-93		46	-

FLETCHER, Mark R. J.

Barnsley, 1st April 1965

Source	Season	Club	Apps.	Gls
App	1983-84	Barnsley	1	-
Tr	1984-85	Bradford C	6	-

FOREMAN, Darren

Southampton, 12th February 1968

From Fareham Town

Source	Season	Club	Apps.	Gls
	1986-87	Barnsley	16	1
	1987-88		9	4
	1988-89		5	-
	1989-90		17	3
Tr	1989-90	Crewe Alex	14	3
	1990-91		9	1
Tr	1990-91	Scarborough	14	5
	1991-92		24	2
	1992-93		42	27

FUTCHER, Paul

Chester, 25th September 1956

Source	Season	Club	Apps.	Gls
App	1972-73	Chester	2	-
	1973-74		18	-
Tr	1974-75	Luton T	19	-
	1975-76		41	-
	1976-77		40	1
	1977-78		31	-
Tr	1978-79	Manchester C	24	-
	1979-80		13	-
Tr	1980-81	Oldham A	36	1
	1981-82		37	-
	1982-83		25	-
Tr	1982-83	Derby Co	17	-
	1983-84		18	-
Tr	1983-84	Barnsley	10	-
	1984-85		36	-
	1985-86		37	-
	1986-87		36	-
	1987-88		41	-
	1988-89		41	-
	1989-90		29	-
Tr	1990-91	Halifax T	15	-

Source	Season	Club	Apps.	Gls
Tr	1990-91	Grimsby T	22	-
	1991-92		29	-
	1992-93		35	-

FUTCHER, Ronald
Chester, 25th September 1956

Source	Season	Club	Apps.	Gls
App	1973-74	Chester	4	-
Tr	1974-75	Luton T	17	7
	1975-76		31	10
	1976-77		33	13
	1977-78		39	10
Tr	1978-79	Manchester C	17	7
From NAC Breda (Netherlands)				
	1984-85	Barnsley	19	6
	1985-86		40	17
	1986-87		25	13
Tr	1986-87	Bradford C	10	4
	1987-88		32	14
Tr	1988-89	Port Vale	41	17
	1989-90		11	3
Tr	1989-90	Burnley	23	7
	1990-91		34	18
Tr	1991-92	Crewe Alex	21	4

Ron Futcher
(pictured 1984) Ron and his 'identical' twin brother Paul played together at Barnsley for three seasons.
photo courtesy Barnsley Chronicle

GEDDIS, David
Carlisle, 12th March 1958

Source	Season	Club	Apps.	Gls
App	1976-77	Ipswich T	2	-
L	1976-77	Luton T	13	4
	1977-78	Ipswich T	26	4
	1978-79		15	1
Tr	1979-80	Aston Villa	20	2
	1980-81		9	4
	1981-82		14	6
	1982-83		4	-
L	1982-83	Luton T	4	-
Tr	1983-84	Barnsley	31	14
	1984-85		14	10
Tr	1984-85	Birmingham C	18	12
	1985-86		26	6
	1986-87		2	-
L	1986-87	Brentford	4	-
Tr	1986-87	Shrewsbury T	15	5
	1987-88		15	5
	1988-89		9	1
Tr	1988-89	Swindon T	10	3
Tr	1989-90	Darlington	9	3
	1990-91		13	-

GLAVIN, Ronald M.
Glasgow, 27th March 1951

Source	Season	Club	Apps.	Gls
Celtic	1979-80	Barnsley	42	20
	1980-81		37	18
	1981-82		27	7
	1982-83		35	17
	1983-84		35	11
From Belenenses (Portugal)				
(N/C)	1985-86	Barnsley	6	-
Tr (N/C)	1986-87	Stockport Co	10	1

GLOVER, E. Lee
Kettering, 24th April 1970

Source	Season	Club	Apps.	Gls
YT	1987-88	Nottingham F	20	3
L	1989-90	Leicester C	5	1
L	1989-90	Barnsley	8	-
	1990-91	Nottingham F	8	1
	1991-92		16	-
L	1991-92	Luton T	1	-
	1992-93	Nottingham F	14	-

GODFREY, Warren
Liverpool, 31st March 1973

Source	Season	Club	Apps.	Gls
YT	1991-92	Liverpool	-	-
Tr	1992-93	Barnsley	8	-

GOODISON, C. Wayne
Wakefield, 23rd September 1964

Source	Season	Club	Apps.	Gls
App	1982-83	Barnsley	3	-
	1984-85		12	-
	1985-86		21	-
Tr	1986-87	Crewe Alex	35	-

Source	Season	Club	Apps.	Gls
	1987-88	Crewe Alex	34	-
	1988-89		25	1
Tr	1989-90	Rochdale	45	4
	1990-91		34	-

GRAHAM, Deiniol W. T.

Cannock, 4th October 1969

Source	Season	Club	Apps.	Gls
YT	1987-88	Manchester U	1	-
	1989-90		1	-
Tr	1991-92	Barnsley	21	1
	1992-93		15	1
L	1992-93	Preston NE	8	-

GRAY, Philip

Belfast, 2nd October 1968

Source	Season	Club	Apps.	Gls
App	1986-87	Tottenham H	1	-
	1987-88		1	-
	1988-89		1	-
L	1989-90	Barnsley	3	-
	1990-91	Tottenham H	6	-
L	1990-91	Fulham	3	-
Tr	1991-92	Luton T	14	3
	1992-93		45	19

GRAY, Stuart

Withernsea, 19th April 1960

From Withernsea Y.C.

Source	Season	Club	Apps.	Gls
	1980-81	Nottingham F	14	1
	1981-82		33	2
	1982-83		2	-
L	1982-83	Bolton W	10	-
Tr	1983-84	Barnsley	17	8
	1984-85		7	-
	1985-86		36	2
	1986-87		40	11
	1987-88		20	2
Tr	1987-88	Aston Villa	20	5
	1988-89		35	4
	1989-90		29	-
	1990-91		22	-
Tr	1991-92	Southampton	12	-
	1992-93		-	-

GRIDELET, Philip R.

Hendon, 30th April 1967

Source	Season	Club	Apps.	Gls
Barnet	1990-91	Barnsley	4	-
	1991-92		-	-
	1992-93		2	-
L	1992-93	Rotherham U	9	-

HEDWORTH, Christopher

Wallsend. 5th January 1964

Source	Season	Club	Apps.	Gls
App	1982-83	Newcastle U	4	-
	1984-85		1	-
	1985-86		4	-
Tr	1986-87	Barnsley	20	-

Stuart Gray
Barnsley's Player of the Year 1986-87
celebrating a goal.
photo courtesy Barnsley Chronicle

Source	Season	Club	Apps.	Gls
	1987-88		5	-
Tr	1988-89	Halifax T	11	-
	1989-90		27	-
Tr	1990-91	Blackpool	20	-
	1991-92		4	-

HENDON, Ian

Ilford, 5th December 1971

Source	Season	Club	Apps.	Gls
YT	1989-90	Tottenham H	-	-
	1990-91		2	-
	1991-92		2	-

45

Source	Season	Club	Apps.	Gls
L	1991-92	Portsmouth	4	-
L	1991-92	Leyton Orient	6	-
	1992-93	Tottenham H	-	-
L	1992-93	Barnsley	6	-

HIRST, David E.
Cudworth, 7th December 1967

Source	Season	Club	Apps.	Gls
App	1985-86	Barnsley	28	9
Tr	1986-87	Sheffield W	21	6
	1987-88		24	3
	1988-89		32	7
	1989-90		38	14
	1990-91		41	24
	1991-92		33	18
	1992-93		22	11

HORN, Robert I.
Westminster, 15th December 1961

From Crystal Palace

Source	Season	Club	Apps.	Gls
	1981-82	Barnsley	42	-
	1982-83		20	-
	1983-84		5	-
L	1983-84	Cambridge U	8	-
Tr	1984-85	Crystal Palace	-	-

JACKSON, Chris
Barnsley, 16th January 1976

Source	Season	Club	Apps.	Gls
YT	1992-93	Barnsley	3	-

JEFFELS, Simon
Barnsley, 18th January 1966

Source	Season	Club	Apps.	Gls
App	1983-84	Barnsley	3	-
	1984-85		18	-
	1985-86		11	-
	1986-87		3	-
	1987-88		7	-
L	1987-88	Preston NE	1	-
Tr	1988-89	Carlisle U	29	-
	1990-91		21	3
	1991-92		26	2

JOHNSON, David E.
Liverpool, 23rd October 1951

Source	Season	Club	Apps.	Gls
App	1970-71	Everton	11	1
	1971-72		27	9
	1972-73		12	1
Tr	1972-73	Ipswich T	27	7
	1973-74		40	13
	1974-75		35	9
	1975-76		35	6
Tr	1976-77	Liverpool	26	5
	1977-78		12	3
	1978-79		30	16
	1979-80		37	21
	1981-82		15	2
Tr	1982-83	Everton	31	3

Source	Season	Club	Apps.	Gls
	1983-84		9	1
L	1983-84	Barnsley	4	1
Tr	1983-84	Manchester C	6	1
From Tulsa Rowdies (USA)				
	1984-85	Preston NE	24	3

JONSSON, Siggi
Iceland, 27th September 1966

From I.A. Akranes

Source	Season	Club	Apps.	Gls
	1984-85	Sheffield W	3	-
	1985-86		10	2
L	1985-86	Barnsley	5	-
	1986-87	Sheffield W	13	-
	1987-88		13	1
	1988-89		28	1
Tr	1989-90	Arsenal	6	1
	1990-91		2	-
	1991-92		-	-

JOYCE, Joseph P.
Consett, 18th March 1961

Source	Season	Club	Apps.	Gls
Jnrs	1979-80	Barnsley	8	-
	1980-81		33	-
	1981-82		20	-
	1982-83		32	1
	1983-84		40	1
	1984-85		41	-
	1985-86		40	-
	1986-87		34	-
	1987-88		38	2
	1988-89		45	-
	1990-91		3	-
Tr	1990-91	Scunthorpe U	21	-
	1991-92		40	2
	1992-93		30	-

KIWOMYA, Andrew D.
Huddersfield, 1st October 1967

Source	Season	Club	Apps.	Gls
YT	1985-86	Barnsley	1	-
Tr	1986-89	Sheffield W	-	-
Retired Injury				
	1992-93	Dundee U	21	1

LAW, Nicholas
Greenwich, 8th September 1961

Source	Season	Club	Apps.	Gls
App	1979-81	Arsenal	-	-
Tr	1981-82	Barnsley	19	-
	1982-83		28	-
	1983-84		31	1
	1984-85		35	-
	1985-86		1	-
Tr	1985-86	Blackpool	39	1
	1986-87		27	-
Tr	1986-87	Plymouth A	12	2
	1987-88		26	3
Tr	1988-89	Notts Co	44	4
	1989-90		3	-

Source	Season	Club	Apps.	Gls
L	1989-90	Scarborough	12	-
Tr	1990-91	Rotherham U	32	2
	1991-92		42	-
	1992-93		44	2

LIDDELL, Andrew M.
Leeds, 28th June 1973

Source	Season	Club	Apps.	Gls
YT	1990-91	Barnsley	-	-
	1991-92		1	-
	1992-93		21	2

LOWE, Simon, J.
Westminster, 26th December 1962

From Ossett Town

Source	Season	Club	Apps.	Gls
	1983-84	Barnsley	2	-
Tr	1984-85	Halifax T	42	12
	1985-86		35	7
Tr	1986-87	Hartlepool U	14	1
Tr	1986-87	Colchester U	26	7
	1987-88		10	1
Tr	1987-88	Scarborough	16	3

LOWNDES, Stephen R.
Cwmbran, 17th June 1960

Source	Season	Club	Apps.	Gls
Jnrs	1977-78	Newport Co	5	-
	1978-79		43	8
	1979-80		46	7
	1980-81		40	9
	1981-82		31	3
	1982-83		43	12
Tr	1983-84	Millwall	20	3
	1984-85		37	7
	1985-86		39	6
Tr	1986-87	Barnsley	15	1
	1987-88		44	9
	1988-89		33	6
	1989-90		24	4
Tr	1990-91	Hereford U	17	1
	1991-92		32	3

MALCOLM, Paul A.
Felling, 11th December 1964

From Durham C.

Source	Season	Club	Apps.	Gls
	1984-85	Rochdale	24	-
Tr	1985-86	Shrewsbury T	-	-
Tr	1986-87	Barnsley	3	-
Tr	1988-89	Doncaster R	34	-

MARSHALL, Colin
Glasgow, 1st November 1969

Source	Season	Club	Apps.	Gls
YT	1988-89	Barnsley	1	-
	1989-90		2	-
	1990-91		1	-
L	1991-92	Wrexham	3	-
L	1991-92	Scarborough	4	1

MAY, Lawrence C.
Sutton Coldfield, 26th December 1958

Source	Season	Club	Apps.	Gls
App	1976-77	Leicester C	1	-
	1977-78		5	-
	1978-79		36	4
	1979-80		42	4
	1980-81		34	-
	1981-82		34	3
	1982-83		35	1
Tr	1983-84	Barnsley	41	1
	1984-85		23	1
	1985-86		36	-
	1986-87		22	1
Tr	1986-87	Sheffield W	13	-
	1987-88		18	1
Tr	1988-89	Brighton & HA	24	3

MacDONALD, John
Glasgow, 15th April 1961

Source	Season	Club	Apps.	Gls
	1986-87	Charlton A	2	-
Tr	1986-87	Barnsley	25	7
	1987-88		33	7
	1988-89		32	5
	1989-90		4	1
Tr	1989-90	Scarborough	29	5

McCARTHY, Michael J.
Barnsley, 7th February 1959

Source	Season	Club	Apps.	Gls
App	1977-78	Barnsley	46	1
	1978-79		46	2
	1979-80		44	1
	1980-81		43	1
	1981-82		42	1
	1982-83		39	1
	1983-84		12	-
Tr	1983-84	Manchester C	24	1
	1984-85		39	-
	1985-86		38	-
	1986-87		39	1
Tr	1987-89	Celtic	48	-
Lyon	1989-90	Millwall	6	-
	1990-91		12	-
	1991-92		17	2
	1992-93		-	-

McGUGAN, Paul J.
Glasgow, 17th July 1964

From Eastercraigs

Source	Season	Club	Apps.	Gls
	1983-88	Celtic	49	2
Tr	1987-88	Barnsley	29	1
	1988-89		20	1
Tr	1990-91	Chesterfield	22	1
	1991-92		37	3
	1992-93		13	2

Source	Season	Club	Apps	Gls

McGUIRE, Michael J.
Blackpool, 4th September 1952

Source	Season	Club	Apps	Gls
Jnrs	1971-72	Coventry C	26	1
	1972-73		17	-
	1973-74		24	-
	1974-75		5	-
Tr	1974-75	Norwich C	16	2
	1975-76		30	2
	1977-78		11	-
	1978-79		24	-
	1979-80		19	2
	1980-81		28	3
	1981-82		39	2
	1982-83		15	-
Tr	1982-83	Barnsley	7	1
	1983-84		36	5
	1984-85		4	-
Tr	1984-85	Oldham A	20	1
	1985-86		40	2

McKENZIE, Ian E.
Wallsend, 22nd August 1966

Source	Season	Club	Apps	Gls
App	1985-86	Barnsley	1	-
Tr	1986-87	Stockport Co	30	-
	1987-88		12	-
	1988-89		17	-

O'CONNELL, Brendan J.
Lambeth, 12th November 1966

Source	Season	Club	Apps	Gls
YT	1984-86	Portsmouth	-	-
Tr	1986-87	Exeter C	42	8
	1987-88		39	11
Tr	1988-89	Burnley	43	13
	1989-90		21	4
L	1989-90	Huddersfield T	11	1
Tr	1989-90	Barnsley	11	2
	1990-91		45	9
	1991-92		36	4
	1992-93		40	6

OGLEY, Mark A.
Barnsley, 10th March 1967

Source	Season	Club	Apps	Gls
App	1985-86	Barnsley	2	-
	1986-87		17	-
L	1987-88	Aldershot	8	-
Tr	1987-88	Carlisle U	3	-
	1988-89		26	-
	1989-90		4	1
Tr	1989-90	Aldershot	28	-
	1990-91		34	-
	1991-92		31	1

OWEN, Gordon
Barnsley, 14th June 1959

Source	Season	Club	Apps	Gls
Jnrs	1976-77	Sheffield W	1	-
	1977-78		2	-
	1978-79		22	3
	1979-80		4	1
L	1979-80	Rotherham U	9	-
	1980-81	Sheffield W	6	-
	1981-82		6	-
L	1982-83	Doncaster R	9	-
L	1982-83	Chesterfield	6	2
Tr	1983-84	Cardiff C	39	14
Tr	1984-85	Barnsley	36	14
	1985-86		32	11
Tr	1986-87	Bristol C	35	5
	1987-88		18	6
L	1987-88	Hull C	3	-
Tr	1987-88	Mansfield T	17	3
	1988-89		41	5
Tr	1989-90	Blackpool	28	4
	1990-91		1	-
L	1990-91	Carlisle U	5	-
L	1990-91	Exeter C	4	-

PEARSON, John S.
Sheffield, 1st September 1963

Source	Season	Club	Apps	Gls
App	1980-81	Sheffield W	15	4
	1981-82		24	7
	1982-83		30	7
	1983-84		27	4
	1984-85		9	2
Tr	1985-86	Charlton A	42	14
	1986-87		19	1
Tr	1986-87	Leeds U	18	4
	1987-88		28	6
	1988-89		33	1
	1989-90		7	-
	1990-91		13	1
L	1990-91	Rotherham U	11	5
Tr	1991-92	Barnsley	10	1
L	1991-92	Hull C	15	-
	1992-93	Barnsley	22	3

PICKERING, Michael J.
Heckmondwike, 29th September 1956

Source	Season	Club	Apps	Gls
Jnrs	1974-75	Barnsley	14	-
	1975-76		41	-
	1976-77		45	1
Tr	1977-78	Southampton	41	-
	1978-79		3	-
Tr	1978-79	Sheffield W	35	-
	1979-80		32	-
	1980-81		15	-
	1981-82		24	1
	1982-83		4	-
L	1983-84	Norwich C	1	-
L	1983-84	Bradford C	4	-
L	1983-84	Barnsley	3	-
Tr	1983-84	Rotherham U	24	-
	1984-85		32	1
	1985-86		46	-
Tr	1986-87	York C	32	1
Tr	1987-88	Stockport Co	8	-
	1988-89		8	-

PLUMMER, Calvin A.
Nottingham, 14th February 1963

Source	Season	Club	Apps.	Gls
App	1981-82	Nottingham F	9	2
	1982-83		3	-
Tr	1982-83	Chesterfield	28	7
Tr	1983-84	Derby Co	27	3
Tr	1983-84	Barnsley	2	1
	1984-85		26	2
	1985-86		23	3
	1986-87		3	-
Tr	1987-88	Nottingham F	8	2
Tr	1988-89	Plymouth A	23	1
Tr	1989-90	Chesterfield	44	8

RAMMELL, Andrew V.
Nuneaton, 10th February 1967

Source	Season	Club	Apps.	Gls
From Atherstone United				
	1989-90	Manchester U	-	-
Tr	1990-91	Barnsley	40	12
	1991-92		37	8
	1992-93		30	7

REDFEARN, Neil D.
Dewsbury, 20th June 1965

Source	Season	Club	Apps.	Gls
From Apprentice, Nottingham Forest				
	1982-83	Bolton W	10	-
	1983-84		25	1
L	1983-84	Lincoln C	10	1
Tr	1984-85	Lincoln C	45	4
	1985-86		45	8
Tr	1986-87	Doncaster R	46	14
Tr	1987-88	Crystal Palace	42	8
	1988-89		15	2
Tr	1988-89	Watford	12	2
	1989-90		12	1
Tr	1989-90	Oldham A	17	2
	1990-91		45	14
Tr	1991-92	Barnsley	36	4
	1992-93		46	3

REES, Anthony A.
Merthyr Tydfil, 1st August 1964

Source	Season	Club	Apps.	Gls
From Apprentice, Aston Villa				
Tr	1983-84	Birmingham C	25	2
	1984-85		9	2
	1985-86		8	2
L	1985-86	Peterborough U	5	2
L	1985-86	Shrewsbury T	2	-
	1986-87	Birmingham C	30	4
	1987-88		23	4
Tr	1987-88	Barnsley	14	2
	1988-89		17	1
Tr	1989-90	Grimsby T	35	13
	1990-91		36	10
	1991-92		23	5
	1992-93		31	5

RHODES, Andrew C.
Askern, 23rd August 1964

Source	Season	Club	Apps.	Gls
App	1983-84	Barnsley	31	-
	1984-85		5	-
Tr	1985-86	Doncaster R	30	-
	1986-87		41	-
	1987-88		35	-
Tr	1987-88	Oldham A	11	-
	1988-89		27	-
	1989-90		31	-
Tr	1990-92	Dunfermline	79	-
Tr	1992-93	St. Johnstone	44	-

RIMMER, Stuart A.
Southport, 12th October 1964

Source	Season	Club	Apps.	Gls
App	1981-82	Everton	2	-
	1983-84		1	-
Tr	1984-85	Chester C	24	14
	1985-86		18	16
	1986-87		38	13
	1987-88		34	24
Tr	1987-88	Watford	9	1
	1988-89		1	-
Tr	1988-89	Notts Co	4	2
Tr	1988-89	Walsall	20	8
	1989-90		41	10
	1990-91		27	13
Tr	1990-91	Barnsley	15	1
Tr	1991-92	Chester C	44	3
	1992-93		43	20

ROBINSON, Jamie
Liverpool, 26th February 1972

Source	Season	Club	Apps.	Gls
YT	1991-92	Liverpool	-	-
Tr	1992-93	Barnsley	8	-

ROBINSON, Mark J.
Rochdale, 21st November 1968

Source	Season	Club	Apps.	Gls
YT	1985-86	West Brom A	1	-
	1986-87		1	-
Tr	1987-88	Barnsley	3	-
	1988-89		18	2
	1989-90		24	-
	1990-91		22	1
	1991-92		41	2
	1992-93		29	1
Tr	1992-93	Newcastle U	9	-

ROLPH, Darren G.
Romford, 19th November 1968

Source	Season	Club	Apps.	Gls
From King's Lynn				
	1987-88	Barnsley	2	-

Source	Season	Club	Apps.	Gls

RONSON, William

Fleetwood, 22nd January 1957

Source	Season	Club	Apps.	Gls
App	1974-75	Blackpool	2	-
	1975-76		19	2
	1976-77		41	4
	1977-78		34	3
	1978-79		32	3
Tr	1979-80	Cardiff C	41	2
	1980-81		42	1
	1981-82		7	1
Tr	1981-82	Wrexham	32	1
Tr	1982-83	Barnsley	39	1
	1983-84		39	2
	1984-85		40	-
	1985-86		2	-
L	1985-86	Birmingham C	2	-
Tr	1985-86	Blackpool	3	-

SAVILLE, Andrew V.

Hull, 12th December 1964

Source	Season	Club	Apps.	Gls
Local	1983-84	Hull C	1	-
	1984-85		4	1
	1985-86		9	1
	1986-87		35	9
	1987-88		31	6
	1988-89		20	1
Tr	1988-89	Walsall	12	4
	1989-90		26	1
Tr	1989-90	Barnsley	15	3
	1990-91		45	12
	1991-92		22	6
Tr	1991-92	Hartlepool U	1	-
	1992-93		36	13
Tr	1992-93	Birmingham C	10	7

SEMLEY, Alan

Barnsley, 21st February 1966

Source	Season	Club	Apps.	Gls
App	1983-84	Barnsley	4	-

SHOTTON, Malcolm

Newcastle, 16th February 1957

From Nuneaton Borough

Source	Season	Club	Apps.	Gls
	1980-81	Oxford U	38	5
	1981-82		40	4
	1982-83		46	1
	1983-84		43	1
	1984-85		42	1
	1985-86		42	-
	1986-87		11	-
	1987-88		1	-
Tr	1987-88	Portsmouth	10	-
Tr	1987-88	Huddersfield T	14	-
	1988-89		2	1
Tr	1988-89	Barnsley	37	5
	1989-90		29	1
Tr	1989-90	Hull C	16	2
	1990-91		26	-

Source	Season	Club	Apps.	Gls
	1991-92		17	-

SMITH, Mark C.

Sheffield, 21st March 1960

Source	Season	Club	Apps.	Gls
App	1977-78	Sheffield W	2	-
	1978-79		21	-
	1979-80		44	9
	1980-81		41	1
	1981-82		41	-
	1982-83		41	2
	1983-84		27	2
	1984-85		36	2
	1985-86		13	-
	1986-87		16	-
Tr	1987-88	Plymouth A	41	6
	1988-89		35	-
	1989-90		6	-
Tr	1989-90	Barnsley	25	3
	1990-91		27	6
	1991-92		38	1
	1992-93		4	-
Tr	1992-93	Notts Co	5	-
L	1992-93	Chesterfield	6	1
L	1992-93	Huddersfield T	5	-
L	1992-93	Port Vale	6	-

TAGGART, Gerald P.

Belfast, 18th October 1970

Source	Season	Club	Apps.	Gls
YT	1988-89	Manchester C	11	1
	1989-90		1	-
Tr	1989-90	Barnsley	21	2
	1990-91	Barnsley	30	2
	1991-92		38	3
	1992-93		44	4

THOMAS, D. Gwyn

Swansea, 26th September 1957

Source	Season	Club	Apps.	Gls
App	1974-75	Leeds U	1	-
	1976-77		7	1
	1977-78		3	1
	1978-79		2	-
	1979-80		3	-
	1980-81		2	-
	1981-82		15	-
	1982-83		39	1
	1983-84		17	-
Tr	1983-84	Barnsley	13	-
	1984-85		40	1
	1985-86		39	5
	1986-87		40	5
	1987-88		42	4
	1988-89		24	2
	1989-90		3	-
Tr	1989-90	Hull C	11	-
	1990-91		11	-
Tr	1991-92	Carlisle U	37	1

Source	Season	Club	Apps.	Gls

TILER, Carl
Sheffield, 11th February 1970

YT	1987-88	Barnsley	1	-
	1988-89		4	-
	1989-90		21	1
	1990-91		45	2
Tr	1991-92	Nottingham F	26	1
	1992-93		37	-

WALSH, Ian P.
St. Davids, 4th September 1958

App	1976-77	Crystal Palace	1	-
	1977-78		16	2
	1978-79		33	8
	1979-80		29	6
	1980-81		25	5
	1981-82		13	2
Tr	1981-82	Swansea C	5	2
	1982-83		8	3
	1983-84		24	6
Tr	1984-85	Barnsley	16	-
	1985-86		33	15
Tr	1986-87	Grimsby T	30	9
	1987-88		11	5
Tr	1987-88	Cardiff C	6	-
	1988-89		11	4

WARDLE, Ian S.
Doncaster, 27th March 1970

Jnrs	1989-90	Barnsley	9	-

WATSON, David
Barnsley, 10th November 1973

YT	1992-93	Barnsley	5	-

WHITEHEAD, Philip M.
Halifax, 17th December 1969

YT	1986-87	Halifax T	12	-
	1988-89		11	-
	1989-90		19	-
Tr	1989-90	Barnsley	-	-
L	1990-91	Halifax T	9	-
	1991-92	Barnsley	3	-
L	1991-92	Scunthorpe U	8	-
	1992-93	Barnsley	13	-
L	1992-93	Scunthorpe U	8	-
L	1992-93	Bradford C	6	-

WHITEHOUSE, Dean
Mexborough, 3rd October 1963

App	1983-84	Barnsley	2	-
Tr	1984-85	Torquay U	9	-

WHITWORTH, Neil A.
Wigan, 12th April 1972

YT	1989-90	Wigan A	2	-
Tr	1990-91	Manchester U	1	-
L	1991-92	Preston NE	6	-
L	1991-92	Barnsley	11	-

WILKES, David A.
Barnsley, 10th March 1964

App	1981-82	Barnsley	2	-
	1982-83		4	-
L	1982-83	Halifax T	4	-
	1983-84	Barnsley	11	2
From Hong Kong				
	1986-87	Stockport Co	8	-
From Hong Kong				
	1990-91	Carlisle U	1	-
From Bridlington Town				
	1991-92	Carlisle U	4	-

WILLIAMS, Gareth A.
Cowes (I.O.W), 12th March 1967

From Gosport Borough				
	1987-88	Aston Villa	1	-
	1988-89		1	-
	1989-90		10	-
Tr	1991-92	Barnsley	17	-
	1992-93		8	5
L	1992-93	Hull C	4	-

WYLDE, Rodger J.
Sheffield, 8th March 1954

App	1972-73	Sheffield W	3	1
	1974-75		12	-
	1975-76		21	1
	1976-77		44	21
	1977-78		36	9
	1978-79	Sheffield W	38	14
	1979-80		15	8
Tr	1979-80	Oldham A	10	4
	1980-81		29	12
	1981-82		35	16
	1982-83		39	19
From Sporting Lisbon				
	1984-85	Sunderland	11	3
Tr	1984-85	Barnsley	17	4
	1986-87		15	7
	1987-88		20	8
L	1987-88	Rotherham U	6	1
Tr	1988-89	Stockport Co	26	12

Supporters' Guides : -

THE SUPPORTERS' GUIDE TO PREMIER & FOOTBALL LEAGUE CLUBS 1994

Featuring :
- all Premier League Clubs
- all Football League clubs
+ 1992/93 season's Results & Tables
120 pages - price £4.99 - post free

THE SUPPORTERS' GUIDE TO NON-LEAGUE FOOTBALL 1994

Featuring :
- all GM/Vauxhall Conference clubs
- all HFS Loans - Premier clubs
- all Beazer Homes - Premier clubs
- all Diadora Premier clubs
+ 180 other major Non-League clubs
112 pages - price £4.99 - post free

THE SUPPORTERS' GUIDE TO SCOTTISH FOOTBALL 1994

Featuring :
- all Scottish League clubs
- all Highland League clubs
- all East of Scotland League clubs
+ Results, tables
96 pages - price £4.99 - post free

THE SUPPORTERS' GUIDE TO WELSH FOOTBALL 1994

Featuring :
- all Konica League of Wales clubs
- all Cymru Alliance & Abacus League clubs
+ 'The Exiles', Minor League clubs & 1992/93 season's results and tables
96 pages - price.£4.99 - post free

order from : -

**SOCCER BOOK PUBLISHING LTD.
72 ST. PETERS AVENUE
CLEETHORPES
DN35 8HU
ENGLAND**